MARRYING SANTIAGO

MARRYING SANTIAGO

A Peace Corps Writers Book/An imprint of Peace Corps Worldwide
Copyright © 2015 by Suzanne Adam
All rights reserved.

For more information, contact peacecorpsworldwide@gmail.com.
Peace Corps Writers and the Peace Corps Writers colophon are
trademarks of PeaceCorpsWorldwide.org.

Book design and production by Marian Haley Beil
Illustrations by Nicolás Gordon
Cover photo by Juan Pablo Calabi

PERMISSIONS

Page 106: "The Morning with Oscar" was previously published in the
Christian Science Monitor.

Page 154: From THE COLLECTED POETRY OF ROBINSON JEFFERS, VOLUME 3, 1939–1962,
edited by Tim Hunt. Copyright (©) "The Double Axe," 1948 by Robinson Jeffers,
1975 Garth and Donnan Jeffers. All rights reserved.
Used with the permission of Stanford University Press, www.sup.org.

Page 156: From WHERE THE BLUEBIRD SINGS TO THE LEMONADE SPRINGS, "Thoughts
in a Dry Land" by Wallace Stegner, Random House LLC.

Page 160: *La Orden Franciscana de Chile autoriza el uso de la obra de
Gabriela Mistral. Lo equivalente a los derechos de autoría son entregados a la
Orden Franciscana de Chile, para los niños de Montegrande y de Chile,
de conformidad a la voluntad de Gabriela Mistral.*

ISBN: 978-1-935925-53-8
Library of Congress Control Number: 2014957255

First Peace Corps Writers Edition, May 2015

MARRYING SANTIAGO

Suzanne Adam

A PEACE CORPS WRITERS BOOK

Prologue

Santiago, Chile. 1989.

I handed the airport customs agent my sworn statement declaring I was carrying no plants, seeds or fresh foods into the country. The official waved me through. Outside, I patted the bulge in my pocket — a plastic tube containing a ten-inch California redwood seedling, a living keepsake. I wouldn't do that now. Those were times of relative ecological innocence, and biodiversity was not yet a word in my vocabulary.

In my walled city garden I looked about for a protected spot to plant the redwood. Maybe in the opposite corner from the avocado tree my son Nicolás started from seed when he was a child. Soon my California wildflowers, iris and blue-eyed grass, would be in bloom along with the Chilean digitalis and wild fuchsia. Sometimes I think that in a previous life I was a Gatherer. On my forays to the countryside, seedpods seem to find their way into my pockets of their own accord.

Choosing a spot, I placed the redwood seedling gently in the hole I'd prepared and thought about the roots I'd put down in Chile over the years. I wondered how deep these roots reached. Had they found in this dry foreign soil the nourishment necessary for a full, rich existence?

1

Blame It on the Trio Los Panchos

Canciones de Amor

The room, enveloped in a smoky haze of cannabis, vibrated to Santana's guitar. *Oye como va, mi ritmo . . ..* My Afghani friend Zmarak and I stood watching the dancers. He'd invited me to this party at the apartment of three Venezuelan students. He didn't know them, nor did I. Not a problem in Berkeley.

A young man approached and asked me to dance.

His smooth, dark skin, long wavy hair, full moustache and neat goatee lent him a dashing Ché Guevara look. Ché, whose image adorned T-shirts, posters and Berkeley walls in that year of 1971.

"Hi. I'm Santiago."

"I'm Suzanne . . .. Where are you from?"

"From Santiago . . . Chile."

"I lived for two years in Colombia," I told him.

"*Hablas español?*"

"*Sí.*"

"*Qué hacías en Colombia?*"

"I was a Peace Corps volunteer."

He had just finished his Masters degree in engineering. I told him I was teaching a bi-lingual Spanish-English class. When a friend dancing next to us made a comment to him that I didn't understand, I asked, "What did he say?" "*Qué dijo?*"

"No, nothing." "*Nada.*"

Maybe my ears weren't attuned to Chilean Spanish. Just as well I didn't catch it, he later admitted. His friend had told him to grab my butt.

As we danced, he pulled me closer, his cheek against mine. And he hummed in my ear, slightly off-key. It tickled.

Was I programmed from birth to marry a Latino? Certain strong, lasting memories prompt me to consider this question.

Growing up in California, immersed in Spanish place names, like my home town of San Anselmo, the language was familiar and to my young, imaginative mind its culture suggested romantic, distant lands. I'd studied Spanish in high school, where tall, stoop-shouldered Father Cunningham, in his long black cassock, ran the class with dry humor, helping offset the drudgery of looking up in the dictionary the unfamiliar words from *El Sombrero de Tres Picos*.

In the spring break of my freshman year at Berkeley, I travelled with my parents to Mexico. It wasn't only the idyllic setting of Guaymas that bewitched me — the blue- and yellow-tiled pool edged by bright hibiscus, the shimmering Pacific just steps away — but the children calling, "*Mira, mamá*. Look, *Mamá !*"

Lounging in a deck chair, I watched them laugh and splash. I thought to myself: I'd like to be called that someday. "*Mamá.*"

It was in my senior year that I fell for Juan, handsome and fun with teasing eyes and an irresistible Cuban accent. He spoke patiently to me in Spanish, his words flowing rhythmically like the love ballads of the Trio Los Panchos that my friends and I had discovered. I'd bought their LP with its pink and yellow cover and the white-jacketed Trio's smiling faces. We sang along:

"*Ay, ay, ay, ay, canta y no llores . . .*" and dreamed of dark, suave Latinos.

Juan was accepted for graduate school at Stanford. But at twenty-one, I was unsure what I wanted to do. I'd studied political science and Spanish out of interest, but realized I had no marketable skills. High with a sense of adventure I joined the Peace Corps and was sent to Colombia.

I stepped off the plane into humid, dusty, mosquito-ridden Barranquilla, a short distance from the Caribbean coast. After a week, I located in my assigned *barrio* an unoccupied small, cinder block house with no plumbing and giant cockroaches crawling down the walls in the night or flying about erratically, keeping me in constant fear of one landing in my hair.

I lived among mulattos who had learned to sway to the *cumbia* before they learned to walk. Bare-armed brown bodies, sweating in the relentless heat, pressing against me in the crowded streets and buses, awakened every sense in my own body. At the *Mercado Central* the plump, ripe mangoes and guanabanas permeated the air like heady aphrodisiacs. Juan and I wrote often, he starting each letter with *Querida Susanita*.

My barrio neighbors were every color of brown, from café latte to dark chocolate, and eked out their livings in wooden shacks with dirt floors. Faced with their poverty, I felt powerless, yet they welcomed me, inviting me in for a Fanta or whatever was in the pot for lunch. After visiting several homes one afternoon, I was pretty much Fanta-ed out. At the corner shop, *Las Tres Esquinas*, I waited behind Señora Delia while she bought one carrot, an onion and a handful of rice wrapped in newspaper. Another day I watched as the three girls across the street sat in their open doorway picking lice from each other's hair.

I'd become friends with Ana, an impoverished, pretty young mother of three, whose partner had a second family in a different barrio. When I got word that she was ill, I rushed her in a taxi to the best private hospital in the city. Her heart was visibly pounding wildly in her chest. She lost the ability to speak. A kind doctor said he suspected meningitis, but made clear I'd have to move her to the public hospital. Neither her family nor I could afford to keep her where she was. The sight of her dark sad eyes sunken in her emaciated face the last time I saw her is a vision I'll never forget. She died within a few weeks.

Yet, there was Dominga, my cigar-smoking, mulatto housemate, cook, companion and dearest friend who had me laughing even on the hardest days. An illiterate, single mother and now a grandmother, she was proud, morally upright, opinionated and wise. I devoured the fried plantains and stuffed potatoes she prepared for me and practiced the refrains she'd taught her two parrots, perched on a kitchen rafter. "*Lorito real, para la España no, sino para el Portugal.*" Soon I was speaking Spanish with a Caribbean accent like a local.

My Peace Corps stay was nearing its end. Though I'd previously rejected the idea of a teaching career, those barrio days convinced me that as an educator I could make a difference. In the Barranquilla airport, Dominga and I hugged and cried as I prepared to board the plane home. I promised to return.

Back in Berkeley to study for an elementary education degree, reverse culture shock hit me like a Mack truck. Juan stopped calling me. I felt adrift and insecure, even unsure I wanted to teach once I'd earned my degree.

When the opportunity arose to return to Colombia to train new Peace Corps volunteers for two months, I jumped at the chance. I saw Juan once more, telling him of my plans.

Upon returning to Berkeley, I learned the shocking news that Juan had drowned in a tragic rafting accident that summer. He was just 24. I mourned by his hillside grave, telling him I regretted letting us grow apart. The thought haunted me that, if I hadn't gone away, it might never have happened.

I rented a small Berkeley apartment with a distant view of the Bay and took a job substitute teaching. After landing a permanent position for the fall, I traveled one more time to visit

Dominga and then on to Mexico to meet with a friend.

Music was everywhere in Mexico, on buses, in shops and on the streets – the Trio Los Panchos and Spanish crooner Raphael's soulful voice singing "*Hablemos de Amor.*" No wonder I gravitated towards Latin men. They had a way with words. Maybe it was the music of the language. Or the language of the music.

It was in my second year of teaching that I met Santiago. The following weekend he asked me out to a small party hosted by his Chilean friends. He picked me up in his 1962 faded beige Chevy Nova.

Opening the car door for me, he said, "I call her my Maserati."

Inside, he leaned towards me. "Are you cold? Here, I'll turn on the heater."

A gurgling noise from under the dashboard was followed by spurts of warm, rusty water streaming out over my favorite salmon-colored Italian boots.

We entered an apartment filled with lively chatter and laughter. Santiago introduced me around, and each greeted me with a kiss on the cheek and "*Hola, Susana.*"

As Santiago and I talked, I learned that he had competed for Chile in the 400 meter hurdles event at the 1968 Mexican Olympic Games. The needle on my Male Interest Meter shot up.

The following Saturday he took me to my first track meet. Sitting in the stands, I was nervous, but he glided over the hurdles with the ease of a gazelle, enabling me to admire his muscular legs and firm, shapely butt. That evening we joined his friends again, where their warmth and love for their country captivated me. They sang Chilean folk tunes — "*Mi caballo, mi caballo galopando va ...*" — and talked wistfully of "home". I borrowed a record of the Huasos Quincheros, a popular folk group, playing it again and again.

So it was I fell for a Chilean and became enamored of a country I'd never seen.

SUZANNE ADAM

We spent every free moment we could manage between our jobs together. His studies completed, Santiago, while hunting for an engineering position, was putting in a back-bending, eight-hour-day with the Mayflower Moving Company, acquiring an all-American education in truck drivers' lingo. Evenings he worked at Swenson's Ice Cream Shop, where I'd wait for him every night while he mopped the floor and closed up. My bonus was an abundant supply of ice cream.

Walking home in the soft summer nights and on lazy weekend mornings sharing the bulky wall bed of my apartment, we told each other our stories. He'd arrived in Berkeley two years earlier with minimal English and no money. For a year he slept on a daybed in the student apartment of a married Chilean couple, and worked in a Volvo garage, changing oil and mufflers, washing cars and making himself scarce when the union inspector came around. He related his previous travels as an athlete: Argentina, Peru, the Pan American Games in Canada. The first in his family to earn a university degree, he then trained a year in Germany in preparation for the Olympics. In Mexico he came down with the flu, only competing because his teammates pulled him out of bed. Soon after, accepted to study at Berkeley, he sold his few possessions and headed north.

One day, towards summer's end, Santiago said, "I'm not going to work tomorrow. I have to go the Immigration Service in San Francisco."

"You do? Why?"

"They've been calling my apartment for months, but I told my roommates to say I wasn't home. My student visa expired three months ago. They finally contacted me and told me to get myself over there."

"What will you tell them?"

"That I've been hunting for an engineering job — you know how many letters I've sent out."

In their office, an agent told him to pack his bags pronto. He had his degree, and his time on United States soil had come to an end. When he gave me the news, doubts flooded my head. Would he just take off and that'd be the end of it? What about us? Talk of our future was premature, each of us insecure about bringing it up. But the question loomed between us, until finally Santiago suggested I go for a visit to Chile during the Christmas holidays.

On a September morning, six months after we met, I watched his plane taxi down the runway at the San Francisco airport. Earlier, we'd clung to each other, reluctant to let go. He then handed his ticket to the airline attendant and walked down the hallway, turning at the last moment to wave. I suddenly felt very alone and adrift. Could weekly letters and occasional static-ridden phone calls keep our relationship alive? I counted the days until Christmas vacation.

I scanned the disorderly crowd mobbing the Santiago airport's exit door. There, among the bobbing heads and waving hands, I spotted Santiago's face with that beloved walrus moustache. Hugs, kisses, smiles and "Meet my mother," he said, nodding to a small, grey-haired lady next to him.

We drove up to his parents' brick town house situated at the back of an unpaved, U-shaped court of identical units, where Santiago lived. He introduced me to his father, Don Roberto, and then showed me to the small guest room upstairs where I would sleep. Throughout the afternoon, the rest of the family trickled in, everyone curious to meet Santiago's *gringa*. First came his two older sisters, Isabel and Olguita, blonde, blue-eyed and fair-skinned, having inherited the Scottish-English genes of their father, Roberto Gordon, son of a Scottish immigrant. Later that day, came his older brother Roberto, dark-skinned, like Santiago, taking after their mother, Señora Olga. Santiago was the fourth child, followed by younger sister Rosa María, working in Mexico at the time. Cousin Gloria lived next door and joined the parade of visitors. That night in bed my head buzzed with all the names and faces, and I had yet to meet numerous aunts, uncles, cousins, nieces and nephews whose names I would struggle to commit to memory.

Santiago was eager to impress me. We took off in a borrowed car, traveling the width and length of Chile, mountains to coast, then south to lakes and volcanoes. I wondered what his family thought of our traveling together in our unmarried status. The warm summer days, the brown hills and the yellow lupines, so like California, helped me feel at home. My visit reaffirmed our resolve to be together. But where? How?

"I'm afraid I won't find an engineering job if I return to the States," he said. "Remember all those job applications I sent out?"

"I could come back in June," I said, "when the school year ends, quit my job and look for a teaching position here." It didn't feel like a tough decision. I wasn't particularly happy in my current job. I'd lived the independent, free spirit Berkeley life for four years and felt ripe for change. Though it meant waiting six months, we agreed it was the best solution.

Back in Berkeley I sold many of my possessions, including the bed I'd slept in all my life, and put the rest in storage. I told my family I didn't know how long I'd be gone.

On July 14th, 1972, Bastille Day, I returned to Chile — straight into a vortex of political and social turmoil.

(Letter translated from Spanish)

Santiago
October, 1971
Via Air Mail

Mi adorada Susanita,

Today it's been a month since my arrival in Santiago and since our sad parting. I think I'll remember for the rest of my days those last moments with you that Sunday. I felt such anguish that I could have cried an ocean of tears but that would have spoiled our final minutes together. That moment before boarding the plane was the worst. The pain was unbearable. I wanted to grab you and bring you with me.

Back in Chile, after twenty-four sleepless hours, I went to bed exhausted and alone, my first night far from you, without the warmth of your body next to mine, your caresses, your kisses and the games we used to play.

Right now it's 11 p.m. and 8 p.m. in San Francisco. I imagine you sitting on the sofa, barefoot, with your school books preparing your classes for tomorrow. Maybe you're thinking of me as I am thinking of you at this very moment.

I realize, now that I'm alone, just how many things we have in common and that we never stopped to analyze. How I wish you were here at my side to share everything with you.

Perhaps our relationship, this sharing between two people, is one of the things that gives such joy; maybe it's our understanding of the word *love*, something difficult to identify.

The days pass and thoughts come and go in my mind: what could be the ideal solution? How can we complete this missing stage in our relationship? I really don't see a solution that doesn't involve a compromise, a giving in, by one of us. My situation is difficult as you well know; yours is equally difficult. How do I have the right to ask you to give everything up? I beg you to say something, tell me your fears, what you think, how do you imagine that we can resolve this?

2

Just For Now

Por Mientras

A pounding din roared in the distance. Like a metallic wave, the rumble swelled louder, closer. Clang. Clang. Clang. It was my first night in the city, staying with Santiago's sister Isabel in her apartment. I looked at her in bewilderment.

"It's the *cacerolazo*, the protest of the casseroles," she said. "Every night women and children take to their doorsteps and balconies, banging on pots and pans in protest against the food shortages."

The clamor grew, and our street came alive. She rushed to her closet-sized kitchen, grabbed a dented, blackened aluminum pot and a soup ladle and headed to her balcony. The spontaneous, female demonstration of strength and solidarity amazed me. I'd never seen anything like this before. Isabel handed me two pot lids.

I'd arrived early that grey winter morning to Pudahuel Airport on an overnight flight from San Francisco. Santiago borrowed his brother Roberto's car to pick me up. After six long months,

I felt once more his prickly moustache on my lips and inhaled his familiar smell. As we headed uptown, the drabness of the buildings and stores and the bare trees along the Alameda couldn't dampen my spirits.

I was to stay with Isabel — separated from her husband Gustavo — and their dark-eyed, year-old daughter, Isabelita. The apartment was around the block from Santiago's second sister, Olguita, and four blocks from his parents' house. Brother Roberto and his family were just down the street.

Isabel rose early the next morning, bundled up her daughter, and headed out to deliver her to a child-care center on her way to her secretarial job. Santiago stopped by to see me before boarding the bus downtown to his office at a housing cooperative. I was on my own, though he arranged for me to have lunch with Olguita. Mother of two young children, her warmth and simplicity made me feel immediately at ease. After lunch, we sat together to watch "Natacha," the current daytime soap.

Within days I found a temporary job teaching a third grade class at Santiago College, a large, long-established English language school. That first morning I walked into a classroom not that different from those at my old school, St. Anselm's: wood floors and desks, iron radiators and one blackboard at the front of class. It took some minutes for me to settle down my students, a small group of noisy, sweet, undisciplined children, the boys clad in heavy beige overalls and the girls in blue- and white-checked aprons over their navy blue jumpers. I was now "*Mees Suzanne*." The lack of teaching materials meant working during my after-school hours at home making my own — cutting pictures and words from discarded American workbooks, pasting them onto tag board and covering them with plastic.

Evenings, I huddled against the kerosene heater in a corner of Isabel's living room. With limited central heating, every building and home felt cold to me. Isabel, Santiago and I would settle in front of her 12-inch black-and-white television to watch news reports of angry crowds of demonstrators marching up the

Alameda carrying banners and placards, *carabineros* dispersing them with tear gas and water hoses. President Salvador Allende's socialist experiment wasn't going as planned. My memories of those first days are tinted in hues of black and white and gray, like old photographs. Not only were the mid-winter trees, sky and buildings grey. So were the faces.

It was the second year of Allende's term, South America's first socialist president. Elected by a congressional coalition of the Socialist, Communist and Christian Democrat parties, he received just thirty-six percent of the popular vote, triggering an era of unrest and conflict.

I gave little thought to the historical impact of the events occurring around me. My energies were focused on learning Chilean Spanish, finding shoes to fit my size nine feet in a country of tiny-footed women, studying the numbers on the drab-green electric trolley cars and learning my way around town.

Eight years in Berkeley — the era of the Free Speech Movement and anti-Vietnam War demonstrations — didn't prepare me for the massive political unrest I encountered in Chile. I was also slow to understand that Santiago, his family and circle of friends and acquaintances belonged to a homogeneous, like-minded, though not necessarily moneyed, upper echelon, conservative and tightly knit.

Several days passed before Isabel's reference to a "food shortage" took on meaning. What to have for dinner became a daily quest. Having never wanted for anything, I took on this challenge with American-pioneer determination. There was a certain satisfaction in "making do." Not only was there a scarcity of food, but also of staples. The only brand of toilet paper available, "Confort," was dull green and a tad above newspaper in its degree of softness. I wondered if this was like living in the Eastern European countries under Communist regimes. Wanting to be helpful to Isabel, who worked longer hours and had Isabelita to care for, I trudged in my ill-fitting Chilean shoes from store to store, hunting down a chicken, sugar or, if lucky, a piece of meat.

One afternoon a long, snaking line outside the Unicoop supermarket drew me like a hound to a foxhole. My technique — lacking any previous experience — was pure instinct and straightforward: grab a place in line, ask the reason for the line and arm myself with patience. The going was slow. Once finally inside, I pushed and elbowed like all the rest to grab whatever I could. Pushy didn't come easily to me, but what satisfaction to arrive home with a scrawny chicken for dinner.

I soon caught on — get to know your local grocer. A good day was when Don Manuel, the owner of the corner shop, told us regular customers in a hushed voice, "Next Thursday I'll be getting some chickens in." Another day, neighbors spread the word, "They've got cooking oil at the store up the street." Hurrying there, empty bottle in hand, I waited until no customers were around before asking, "*Hay aceite?* Do you have oil?" The clerk escorted me into a back room where he filled my bottle from a large vat of greenish liquid of questionable origin. But who was in a position to question?

I didn't go hungry, but did learn to be satisfied with simple and even unappetizing fare. Rice, vegetables and eggs were readily available. Imported New Zealand lamb, chickens from France, potatoes from the U.S.A and Chinese pork, *chancho chino*, sometimes added variety to our diets. If nothing else was available, we resorted to a Swiss chard omelet. The only problem with this dish . . . the eggs. I had to confront my dislike for eggs, a challenge that stemmed from my childhood when my mother believed that slimy, soft-boiled eggs constituted a healthy breakfast.

At an impromptu dinner at the home of a friend of Santiago's, the hostess brought out the food with an apology. "Forgive the dinner, but it's all we had." She passed us a plate of rice topped with a fried egg. We smiled and reassured her that it was the company that mattered. Occasionally Santiago and I went to our favorite crepe restaurant, Misia Trini, for a change of fare.

We didn't bother to read the menu, but simply asked the waiter, "*Qué hay?*" "What do you have?"

One day Santiago's mother introduced me to a new national pastime. Hoarding. Like a squirrel preparing for fall, she had stuffed her closets with rolls of toilet paper, boxes of tea, and bags of sugar. Like everyone else, she feverishly bought up any non-perishable item in fear of worse times to come. That well-stocked closet gave her a sense of security, enabling her to trade an item from her cache for something she needed. Hoarding and a booming black market led to greater shortages, triggering a nationwide domino effect.

Also in short supply were venues for weekend recreation. The three old movie houses in our part of town showed mainly European films: *Amarcord, Boccaccio 70*. One Sunday Santiago drove me to a small civil airport where we sat and watched the planes taking off and landing.

More entertaining were our Sunday visits to the Montecino's home. Sergio Montecino, a renowned national artist, was the father of Santiago's friend, Cecilia. Having no telephone, we didn't call ahead to announce our coming, but they always welcomed us into their hillside home. We'd arrive at tea time, and they'd add another table to the long one already set up in the living room to accommodate visiting cousins and aunts. Surrounded by Don Sergio's loosely-brushed southern landscapes and family portraits, we'd talk and laugh and listen to stories. I remember him sitting in his big chair, placing vinyl records of classical music on the phonograph. Sometimes his easel was set up on the terrace with a work in progress. We'd stay until dark, reluctant to leave that magical atmosphere.

One October evening, behind the closed door of my bedroom, Santiago and I discussed our living arrangements. Strikes and food scarcity were not our only concerns. I had been living with Isabel for three months while Santiago continued at his parents, four blocks away.

Santiago reasoned, "We can't live together. It's just not done here."

I understood he meant that it wasn't done in his social class. Our options were limited. Then he came out with it. "We could get married." What relief for us both when he spoke those words. We knew that now we were ready for a commitment. Excited, we began to make plans, deciding on a wedding during the Christmas holidays when I thought my mother could get away from her teaching job.

I wrote my parents of our decision. "We plan to marry in Chile as we and all of Santiago's family are here. It's a bit rushed, just two months off, but you'll have time to arrange the trip." I explained we were considering settling in the States, but Santiago needed time to decide, and there was all the paperwork. We couldn't afford a trip to California to marry and then another trip if we decided to return.

In shock, I read my mother's answer: "You and Santiago cannot possibly know how we feel, nor will I attempt to tell you. Just don't expect too much enthusiasm." The news was not unexpected, she said, and their first concern was my happiness. They hardly knew Santiago, she continued, but trusted in my judgment. But my father was suffering from angina and also had a great fear of flying. He felt it too risky to make such a long trip. My mother refused to come without him, leaving him alone at Christmas. I had expected my father would be unhappy with our decision to marry in Chile. He feared losing me — but not come to my wedding?

Unlike him, he wrote me two letters within a few weeks. He told of finding my mother crying, "I never thought I'd not be attending my only daughter's wedding." He encouraged her to come alone, but she refused. I wrote my father that his health was most important and he had to decide what was best for him.

Letters flew back and forth. My father consulted his doctor about the wisdom of the trip. My mother began checking out flights. In her next letter she asked where they could stay — if they came. We rushed to make reservations at the Sheraton and find a priest to perform the ceremony.

My father survived the flight and both parents lived through all the introductions. Santiago's family dusted off their rusty English skills, except for Señora Olga and Don Roberto. My mother's limited Spanish and our translations provided the only means of communication between our parents. There was much smiling and head nodding.

The austere times and our limited budget, as well as our own tastes, called for a simple wedding. At a small shop, I found a long white cotton eyelet dress with a scoop neck trimmed with green velvet ribbon. Santiago's mother took me to the home of a woman who made a cluster of white cloth flowers for my hair. His sisters bought flowers at the Mercado Central and arranged them on the altar of the modern chapel at Verbo Divino, a boys' school in the neighborhood.

Gustavo, Isabel's husband — they would soon be reunited — drove my father and me in his Peugeot the two blocks to church. Our photographer was Santiago's friend, Marcelo, who scurried about the chapel in an outrageous orange sports coat. We left the choice of music up to another friend — I don't remember his name — who volunteered to play the organ. It was a small affair of about forty guests, just Santiago's family and close friends. My parents and two American friends married to Chileans were my only guests. After the ceremony, we celebrated with a champagne and cake reception at the clubhouse on the grounds of Santiago's sports club.

Guests listened in disbelief when I told them my parents were going with us on our honeymoon to the coast. "How can we leave them alone in Santiago," I said, "after they traveled all that distance to be with us?" The four of us drove to Zapallar, my favorite beach town, in Santiago's brother's 1964 red and white Opel. My parents said nothing of the plain accommodations at the fading Gran Hotel, or of the meager offerings at the restaurant. They seemed to be enjoying themselves. I sensed they appreciated that we were sharing this time with them.

Back in Santiago, we showed them our married living arrangements. Señora Olga had moved into the guest room, giving us her larger bedroom, now furnished with the two childhood beds once belonging to Santiago and his brother.

"This is just temporary," I assured my parents. "Rentals are scarce and expensive right now." They said nothing.

Their two-week visit came to an end and we saw them off at the airport, reassuring them that we'd be seeing them soon, after I finished the school semester. The dreary economic scene and growing civil strife had convinced us to try our fortunes in the States. That promise, I hoped, mitigated the pain of separation and their worry for my welfare.

Soon after, in a step towards greater independence, we bought our first car, a red Fiat 600. To obtain a new car, Santiago had signed up seven months earlier on the official government list. Fiats were the only cars being assembled in Chile, and deciding on a color was no problem. You took what you got. Most cars on the road then, including old model American cars, sleek with pointy tail fins and weighted with pounds of chrome, would have wound up in a junk yard or an antique car show in the States.

Our Fiat made a Volkswagen Beetle look downright roomy. In January, we took off in *our* red "Bug" to southern Chile on our first summer vacation as a married couple. Passing over the rough dirt roads, we looked and felt like we were driving a vacuum cleaner. Powdered with dust from head to toe, all we could do was laugh. Then, heading back north, a sudden downpour caught us on our way through the town of Temuco, and, in a matter of minutes, water was sloshing around our ankles. Beyond town and out of the cloudburst, Santiago drove off a side road up a low hill. The car manufacturers, apparently foreseeing such emergencies, had provided several rubber plugs under the floor mats. One by one, he pried them out. Voilá!

Out drained the water and we continued on our way. Those discomforts in no way dampened our spirits; after the long wait, we were exuberant at finally having our own wheels.

In March I began teaching a class of second graders at Nido de Aguilas International School. Soon after, an opportunity for greater independence came our way. Debbie, a single American teacher colleague, suggested we three share an apartment. Given the unstable economy and runaway inflation of over three hundred per cent, rents were charged in dollars. Pooling our resources, we rented a large, dark, furnished apartment in an older neighborhood near downtown. The brightest spot in the apartment was our bedroom, wallpapered with a pattern of large, gaudy orange flowers.

At last, on our own.

Well, almost. I wrote my parents that Santiago was well-advanced with the paper work for his U.S. visa. My father agreed to help, filling out forms of detailed financial information in order to be Santiago's sponsor.

Besides, this was just for now. Everything — apartment, jobs, car — was just for now. By the end of the year, we'd be heading back to California.

Santiago

Dear Mother and Daddy,

. . .

July 17, 1972

Here I am in Chile at last. The view from the plane was spectacular, the mountains white with snow. Santiago and his brother came to pick me up.

July 24, 1972

Two weeks. No letter yet from you. I'm anxious for news. Today I went to the Unicoop, a supermarket nearby, to get acquainted with what foods are available. Neither Isabel nor her maid are great cooks, so Santiago has encouraged me to cook. I don't know many dishes that don't require meat, which is very scarce. After a long search, I found canned tuna, so tonight I'll make a tuna casserole.

August 1, 1972

I guess you're wondering what I've decided about my job in Union City. I came here to be with Santiago so that we'd have time together to decide if we want to get married. I don't know how much time we'll need. I can't commute back and forth, so I won't be back for my job.

Santiago talks about working in the States for a while to save some dollars. (The dollar goes a long way here.) I'd rather be in the States than here, to be near you and my friends, but that's a ways in the future.

September 9, 1972

I make roughly sixty dollars a month. It is impossible to live independently on that salary here. At a teachers' meeting at school today we voted on whether or not to join the general strike occurring across Chile.

We don't get much news from the States here and I miss it. The newspapers carry a few items about Nixon's activities and the television shows news footage about Vietnam, but not from the American viewpoint.

November 27, 1972

I was thrilled to read in your letter that you're considering the possibility of coming to our wedding.

January 12, 1973

With the leftover escudos you gave us at the airport, we bought a Sony AM-FM radio that works on electricity or batteries. We enjoy having it in our little room.

3

Times of Change

Momentos de Cambio

September 11, 1973.

Someone heard it on the morning news. The Chilean navy had positioned ships in the harbor of Valparaiso. Outside my classroom door, three of us teachers speculated in whispers. Could this be what we'd all feared — the start of civil war? We had no radios or televisions in our classrooms. There'd been no word from the school administration office at the other end of the building.

I peeked in to check on my class. Unable to focus on teaching, I'd given my small students a dittoed sheet of word puzzles to work on. Their little antennae, no doubt, picked up that something was unusual that morning. I turned back to my companions just as the hall door to our wing swung open. It was the school principal.

"The children are to be sent home. Prepare them and yourselves quickly. Some parents have already arrived; otherwise, the children are to take their regular buses."

SUZANNE ADAM

"But, what's going on?" we asked.

"There's been a military uprising," he said. "A national curfew is to begin at 11 a.m., so move fast."

Back in my classroom, I said, "Girls and boys, listen carefully. Put away your things. You're going home early today. Get your coats and backpacks and line up at the door. Come on. Quickly!" I walked them to the parking lot, making sure they got to their buses or met with their parents.

The morning's events were not a complete surprise to us. Every night for months Santiago and I had followed the news of the growing general strike of factory workers, truck drivers, office clerks and professionals. He, himself, hadn't gone to work for days. The city was a ghost of its former bustling self. A few workers stood on street corners waiting in vain for the exhaust-spewing, multi-colored buses. I was spending more and more time making the rounds to the different corner shops in search of something to eat besides eggs, Swiss chard and rice. Ours was one of the few schools that had remained open. Front page newspaper photos depicted angry, shouting crowds, brandishing banners, marching through city streets, hurling Molotov cocktails at the carabineros. A hidden weapon cache was discovered at the coast, fueling the fears of civil war.

City streets were strangely empty as I drove the long route home from school. As I turned the key in the lock, Santiago rushed to the door, relief written on his face.

"What's going on?" I asked.

He'd been listening to the radio. "It sounds like the military are attempting a take-over, but it's all very unclear. Some of the stations are off the air. Others broadcast military marches and periodic bulletins."

There was nothing for us to do but listen to the radio, wait and speculate. Unable to sit still, he said, "I think I'll walk to the corner to see what's happening." Our apartment was just a block from Avenida Providencia, the main thoroughfare leading to downtown.

"Be careful," I warned and then watched from the window. The minutes ticked by. What was keeping him?

Finally, his footsteps on the stairs and the key in the lock.

"Did you see anything?" I asked.

"Army trucks, loaded with armed soldiers, rolling past towards the center of town. Then, a bullet whizzed over my head, shattering the dry cleaner's sign above me. I thought I'd better get home."

Glued to the radio, on some stations we heard Allende declare that he would not move from *La Moneda*, the presidential palace. At the sudden roar of droning planes low overhead, we raced up the stairs to the top of our apartment building and climbed a small ladder to the roof of a structure housing a water tank. We lay flat and watched.

"They're Air Force Hawker Hunters," said Santiago. The planes circled, diving in low over the heart of the city, followed by thundering blasts and billowing clouds of smoke.

"They're bombing La Moneda!" said Santiago.

The scene seemed unreal. But this was no movie.

When the bombing ceased, an eerie calm followed. We returned to listening to the radio, our only contact with what was occurring beyond our locked door. News was confusing. Military marches, interrupted by bulletins announcing a take-over by the armed forces, continued on some stations, while others remained silent. A state of siege and an around-the-clock curfew were declared throughout the country.

Darkness descended in a curtain of silence. But, then . . . the sound of a motor on our narrow street. A large vehicle. We turned off the lights, crouched low and peered through the window. An army bus pulled up in front of the building across from us. Soldiers emerged and entered the building. Who or what were they looking for? A short while later, they left empty-handed. Sniper and machine gun fire interrupted our fitful sleep throughout the night. Who was doing the shooting? Who was being shot at? The worst was the uncertainty.

SUZANNE ADAM

The next morning we learned from the radio that the military was in control. The official version stated that Allende killed himself in La Moneda, while rumors claimed he was shot or killed in the bombing. The daytime curfew was rescinded, and I ventured out to a nearby shop. Fatigue-clad soldiers, armed with submachine guns, patrolled the streets. Though the soldiers themselves didn't look threatening, I was anxious passing in front of hair-triggered weapons held by nervous hands. Yet, it seemed that the worst was over.

It was difficult to tease out the rumors from the facts, facts fed to us by the military-controlled news. The national anthem often interrupted radio programs. Another announcement. We changed stations, but all transmitted the same official proclamations.

Some newspapers were allowed to circulate again. Articles made reference to suspicious foreigners, young people of leftist persuasion, who came to Chile to support a violent revolution. Reports asserted that some 13,000 Cubans were in the country. Fidel Castro had come for a week-long state visit the year before and stayed a month.

Having been in the country just over a year, I didn't have a grasp of Chilean politics or the background leading up to the coup. I didn't feel directly involved. This wasn't my country, I reasoned. I believed I was an objective observer, but it was difficult to remain impartial. Opinions of family and friends influenced me. When Santiago returned to Chile from the States, he had an open mind towards the newly-elected socialist president and held hopes for a better future for his country. But he quickly became disillusioned with the ranting of politicians, government-supported take-overs of private industries and farms, and the constant strikes and shortages. By the time the coup occurred, he, his family, and our friends and acquaintances fully supported the military. It seemed that it was either that or civil war.

After a few days, I could almost hear a collective sigh of relief. Finally, an end to the strikes, the protest marches, the violence.

We longed to return to normalcy in a society respectful of the law and free of class conflict. And again to eat a piece of meat.

The nighttime curfew became a permanent fixture of our lives. After a dinner one night in the home of Scottish friends, I checked my watch, calculating how long it would take us to get home. As the midnight deadline neared, nervous, I reminded Santiago and the other guests that we had to go. Filing out the door together, we joked about the curfew, hiding our concern for those who had a longer trip home. The dark curfew hours were an anxious time. Every night shots and explosions pierced the unnatural silence. Terrorist opposition to the military had replaced strikes and demonstrations.

Some weeks after the coup, Santiago and I were zipping along in our Fiat, when he declared, "You know . . . I've been thinking. I'd like to stay in Chile for a while to see if the economic situation will improve now."

Just like that. POW! I hadn't seen it coming.

"But, Santiago, the papers for your U.S. visa are almost complete."

He reminded me of his unsuccessful job search in California after graduating. He felt insecure about going through that process again. In Chile he had work.

"We can't live like gypsies, moving back and forth," he said.

"Santiago, we agreed to go to the States as soon as my school semester ends. What am I going to tell my parents? They're expecting us."

"Let's get an economic foothold first. We both have jobs here. And I'd like to have an apartment or something here as an investment. Something to come back to if we return. In the States we'd be starting from scratch."

I was reluctant to argue with Santiago. Since he was to be the major breadwinner, I agreed to give it a try. His reasons sounded legitimate and convincing. Maybe he was right. After all, it wasn't like we were making a lifetime decision. We weren't abandoning the idea of going to the States someday. Focused on the present and lacking the conviction to dissent, I was blind to the implications for our future, that this might be a turning point, or, even — a point of no return.

I leaked the news gradually to my parents, explaining Santiago's reasoning, while reassuring them that we were not ruling out the States and that California was still my preference. I suffered reading my mother's letters: "I can't believe you're really on the planet anymore, the distance being so great. I have a difficult time writing to you. It depresses me, makes me feel desolate." She said my father couldn't bring himself to write me, claimed he didn't read my letters and rarely talked about me to anyone. He had gone to great effort to prepare the financial information to sponsor Santiago and now he'd been duped. Their greatest fear — of losing their daughter — was becoming a reality.

They worried for my safety. The international media was filled with reports of military repression. My mother said to me during one of our infrequent phone calls, "But it's dangerous there. The streets are swarming with armed soldiers."

She talks like the expert and I'm the one living here. "That's an exaggeration," I told her. "It's not as bad as it sounds in the news. I feel perfectly safe here." And I did.

The decision made to give Chile a chance, we began to put down our roots in this land as a family. Just three months after the coup, I learned I was pregnant. Santiago and I shared the news with his family, and I wrote my parents. Their first grandchild, but at the bottom of the world. I wondered if it was due to their disappointment that they chose to go on a European tour around the time of my due date, rather than accept my invitation to come to be with me. Years later I would wonder why I didn't express to them my hurt at their decision.

My maternity leave began with the school's winter break in July and would continue for three months after my due date in August. After much searching, I found a woman who gave La Maze classes. It was clear that my young doctor and Santiago had their doubts. No anesthesia in a country where caesareans were the frequent choice of women who could afford it?

The doctor scheduled a date for an induced birth. It was safer to arrange deliveries and induce babies, rather than run the risk of going out after curfew, and waving a white flag out the car window.

On our way to the hospital on the appointed day, we made a detour to pick up our first television set, a 12-inch black-and-white model. We had signed up for it months earlier on the government list and were now notified that our turn had come up.

At the hospital, I was left to my own devices to follow the La Maze techniques. It was unheard of for a father-to-be to attend the birth of his child, and Santiago was uneasy around the sight of blood. My *matrona*, or midwife, was with me during most of my labor, but wasn't trained in the La Maze method and her enthusiasm for my efforts was tepid. But I did it, giving birth to our first son, Daniel. Euphoria swept through me, a natural high I'd never known before.

All of Santiago's family came to visit me in the hospital and to meet Daniel. Santiago sent a telegram to my parents' hotel announcing Daniel's birth. The next day a telegram arrived from Amsterdam: "Congratulations. All our love, Mother and Daddy." I knew their joy was tempered by the pain of separation and distance. In a postcard from Paris my mother wrote: "How I wish I could be there — for many reasons." Then, why wasn't she?

But I had a local support network, Santiago and his family: his mother, his three sisters, and my pediatrician brother-in-law, Gustavo. The elderly great aunts supplied me with beautifully knitted white wool pants, sweaters, booties and blankets. Getting them white again after a bout with diarrhea was out of the question.

I cared for my newborn son according to local wisdom and advice. This was how they had raised their babies. *Don't feed on demand. Best to establish a schedule right off. A geranium leaf in the rectum helps with constipation. Buy a plastic*

*bucket to soak the diapers in the bathroom. Wash the diapers
with Popeye bar soap, followed by a rinse of boiling water.
Babies should sleep on their tummies. Swaddle them in wool
blankets, even on warm days.*

Following the advice not to feed on demand was a mistake. I
was a nervous new mom, my milk supply limited. Danny caught
cold in the first weeks, making breast feeding more stressful.
In his early photos he looked like a miniature old man. But I
heeded Gustavo's instructions; that was the way baby rearing
was done here. Danny needed to gain weight; I would have to
begin bottle feeding.

We snapped photos of Danny's first bath and smile. I tucked
the photos into an envelope alongside my weekly letters to my
parents written on red-and blue-edged, sheer airmail paper that
with luck would arrive ten days later.

With three of us now, apartment sharing with Debbie was
wearing thin for all. Santiago came home one evening with
unexpected news. He'd obtained a loan for the down payment
to buy a small, attached house. We were ecstatic. After a year
and a half of marriage and our first child, finally we'd have a
place of our own.

The house was unoccupied. The shutters dangled from their
hinges and weeds ran unchecked in the garden, but we saw
possibilities. Inside, it was light and airy, and the small backyard
held a grape arbor and an apricot tree. The house was in the
familiar barrio where all Santiago's family lived. That sector
of town was known as the *barrio alto*, the high neighborhood,
because of the way it sloped up into the foothills of the Andes.
The term soon became synonymous with the higher income
end of town.

We gave the house a coat of white paint and one October
day moved in with three-week-old Danny. We furnished it with
borrowed wicker garden furniture recycled into a living room
set, a sagging box spring mattress salvaged from the school

warehouse, our little TV and second-hand items bought at *gringo vende* sales.

Our new abode was comfortable, but spartan. Most shortages and the black market had ended, but we were still limited to the few Chilean-made products available. For heat the following winter, we depended upon our trusty "Comet," a clunky brown apparatus that squatted in a corner of our dining room. Its unsightly metal flue passed up through the ceiling to the second floor, helping to warm the upstairs bedrooms. The acrid odor of the heater's kerosene permeated the house. Every week we hauled two large plastic containers to the gas station and stood in line to buy the kerosene. I hung the day's wash alongside the Comet on a wooden rack, like the one my mother used before the days of clothes dryers.

My mother bought me a subscription to *Country Living* magazine, and I poured over the pages depicting American country decor for ideas to implement in my South American *casa*. I sewed curtains and bedspreads, searched for pieces of used furniture and filled empty spaces in the house with potted plants. It was beginning to feel like home.

One fall day, I went to Isabel's apartment to call my parents from her phone, a process that involved placing the call with the operator first, and then waiting until she called me back. We still had no telephone. There was a shortage of lines and a waiting list of three to four years. The cost would be several hundred dollars.

My mother's faint voice, interrupted by static, accentuated the gaping distance between us. I asked for my father. She called to him, "She wants to talk to you." He took his time to come to the phone.

"I have great news." I told him. "You will get to meet your grandson. Danny and I are coming to visit for Christmas." Our budget was too tight for Santiago to go.

They photographed every moment: bathing Danny, walking him in the stroller, posing with him in front of the Christmas tree. What delight in their faces, and what a relief for me to have four extra hands, not to mention disposable diapers and Gerber baby food. The Chile-California tensions faded and we simply enjoyed every moment — until departure day neared. No one talked of plans to come visit us. My father refused. He didn't tell me directly; my mother clued me in. Chile, not my husband, had taken his only daughter from him. He would not step on Chilean soil again.

At the airport my mother, holding Danny tightly, said. "I hope you don't have too rough a trip. It's such a long flight." Again, small talk, but what was there to say? She was straining to hold back the tears.

Mine fell as the plane lifted off over the Bay.

Santiago
September 10, 1973

Dear Mother and Daddy,

Now the grocery stores have joined the general strike. We're able to get food from friends who have contacts: from one teacher colleague we buy eggs (has her own chickens), from another, oranges and avocados . . .. We're making our own bread. . .. It's amazing how one can adjust to the situation and make do. When the established ways no longer work, new systems grow up.

Santiago
September 11, 1973

Dear Mother and Daddy,

Here is your on-the-spot reporter in downtown Santiago just down from the roof of our apartment where we watched two Air Force jets attacking the Moneda where Allende and his loyal men have sworn to resist. Smoke is rising downtown, and machine gun fire riddles the air. The coup is in progress as I write.

San Anselmo, California
September 15, 1973

Dear Suzie and Santiago,

Can you imagine how helpless we feel to be completely cut-off, except for sketchy news reports telling of planes dropping bombs and thousands killed? Not even short-wave transmission allowed. You wrote you hoped we weren't worrying. My God! Everyone is worrying, especially as to how foreigners fare.

We heard about the lines at the grocery store after the curfew was lifted. Hope you had a stock of extra food in the house. We were mostly concerned about the location of your apartment, so near to downtown. We shall stay close to home at night, hoping for a phone call.

Daddy will never be reconciled to having his only daughter so far away and living in such an unhappy and unfortunate environment. We both feel so sorry about Chile and its tragedy, but, of course, cannot understand your preference for it. I suppose you could write a book about your experiences this week — how very uncertain you all must have felt.

4

Words Not Spoken

Lo Que No Se Dijo

It was summer now in Chile. I was due to return to teaching in the fall, so I focused on enjoying the warm days with four-month-old Danny, homemaking, and tending our small garden. Under military rule, the country was becoming more stable, and I put politics on a secondary plane. Grocery store shelves began to fill up, and I no longer stood in long lines. Colors seeped into the black, white and gray of our lives, although we continued to live sparingly.

Santiago's family's methods of budgeting — washing dishes and clothes in cold water, cutting paper napkins in half, turning off the pilot of the hot water heater at night, reusing tea bags — struck me as exaggerated and even stingy, yet I soon followed suit. Nothing was thrown away. When we bought a new refrigerator, we gave our old one, bought second-hand, to Santiago's parents. Señora Olga frequented a nearby shop that mended runs in her nylon stockings. Heading to the grocery store, I'd take along mesh bags for packing my purchases, since the store charged for theirs. Anything we no longer wanted or needed — a worn tire, a broken wicker chair — was placed outside the house with the garbage. It was gone by morning.

Friends suggested ways to prepare tasty meals from simple, economic ingredients: strata made from bread, cheese and milk, and a hearty soup from the carcass of a roast chicken, which already had provided two nights' dinners. Abundant and inexpensive fruits and vegetables compensated for the lack of other items. When I bumped into Gloria, Santiago's cousin and mother of six, at the supermarket, she pointed to her shopping cart. "I love buying these big bundles of Swiss chard. They fill my cart, giving me the feeling that I've gotten a lot for my money."

I avoided buying *jurel tipo-salmon*, a popular affordable fish among Chileans. No relation to salmon, it was canned mackerel laced with tiny bones. Fresh dogfish shark was a more palatable alternative, which Señora Olga advised me to soak in milk overnight to eliminate its strong ammonia odor. I took advantage of the readily available enormous cabbages, squash and ears of corn, grown to monumental sizes. Bigger meant more for your money, although not necessarily better quality. The few canned foods in the market as well as the absence of any frozen foods meant we prepared all meals from scratch. Soaking lettuce and celery in Clorox to kill bacteria and prevent cholera was another daily chore.

In March, I returned to my teaching job, now to a class of third graders. We hired petite, dark-eyed Sylvia to care for Danny and help with housework during the day. Middle-aged and unmarried, she was loving with Danny and experienced with running a household which eased my worries as I headed for school in the mornings.

The school was set in the foothills, the Andes their backdrop. At the end of summer, the view through my classroom window revealed brown, dry grass and a few scraggly low trees dotting the hills. That winter, I watched silent snow veil the surrounding hills with a delicate white mantle. Then, as spring crept in, a soft fuzz of intense green grass covered the slopes. I took my students walking on the hillside to observe the California poppies — called golden thimbles here — spring's first harbingers. The warmer days, like magic wands, transformed the native *espino*, a squat, drab, thorny tree. Like an ugly duckling, it shyly donned its springtime plumage of pale yellow pompoms, permeating the air with a delicate, sweet fragrance.

My nesting and mothering instincts were stronger than love for my job. At the end of the school year, I gave notice that I would not be returning. I wanted to be home with Danny and have time for homemaking.

I had another reason for quitting.

In each of my classes, there were two or three children who had special needs that I felt unprepared to handle. I learned that the prestigious Universidad Católica offered a three-year, night time post-graduate program for teaching the learning disabled. I applied and was accepted at the top of the list without taking an entrance exam. My University of California teaching degree made me a shoo-in.

The first night I entered the university classroom not knowing a soul, wondering how I'd manage with my Spanish. The group of forty teachers came from both public and private schools in the many socially and economically diverse neighborhoods of the city. Being the only *gringa* in the program, however, granted me immediate status among my classmates. Several teachers, all from private schools, took me under their wings to form a study group, declaring I took excellent notes. Others, from public schools, formed their own groups. We had gravitated to our own comfort levels — a self-imposed, unintentional segregation.

The professors were competent and friendly, and classes entertaining. Most of my classmates were teaching full time and I could imagine the pressure they were experiencing. I was shocked that many carried on conversations while the professor was speaking. More disturbing was the cheating during tests.

True, it was just a few, but I wondered: what could they expect from their students if their teachers cheated?

During winter break, Santiago, Danny and I escaped to the California summertime. This was Santiago's first trip back to the States since his student days. Now, I hoped, my parents would get to know him. They gave over their bedroom to us and tucked a borrowed crib into one corner. All activities centered on Danny — and shopping.

The abundance in the States dazzled us. We checked out the sales in the newspaper and were off. I headed to the Safeway, floating past teeming shelves of old friends: Cheerios, graham crackers, ice cream sandwiches. Could I squeeze a package of English muffins into my suitcase? It was heaven to return to disposable diapers and wipes.

While I roved Safeway's aisles, Santiago cruised Long's Drug Store, his favorite hangout, checking out cameras, sunglasses, brands of aspirin and jumbo bags of Snickers and Milky Way bars. My parents cut out coupons and saved newspaper sale inserts and Land's End catalogues. But they were puzzled. Why this obsessive, time-consuming shopping, time we could be spending with them?

Although usually kept in check, tensions and resentments sometimes surfaced. One night they greeted us with sour faces and angry words when we arrived from the mall late for dinner. "Don't you realize that your mother has been in the kitchen preparing dinner for you?" said my father. I apologized, but Santiago was upset at my parents' reaction and refused to join us at the table. Differing dinner-time expectations on different continents was an issue we'd have to work with.

Our consumer craze included a used 1966 Volkswagon Kleinbus, which Santiago planned to ship to Chile. Though we were just a short distance from the ports of San Francisco and Oakland, the cheapest way to ship it was via New Orleans. Early one morning, we all stood in front of the house and waved good-bye to Santiago as he putted off in the beige camper. He drove for four long days to New Orleans. After a stopover with friends in Los Angeles, he spent two nights sleeping at rest stops in the back of the camper somewhere in Arizona and then in Texas. Calls from pay phones assured us he was well and on schedule. Arriving in New Orleans, he checked into a motel by the airport. Pouring rain and a taxi strike added to his anxiety as he raced to finalize the shipping arrangements and meet up with Danny and me for our return flight to Chile.

Inside our plane at the New Orleans airport, I scanned the faces of the boarding passengers. Finally, there he came down the aisle, a smile of relief on his face. All that for a VW camper.

Santiago had lived in the States and understood my desire to study and work. We'd met when I was independent and self-supporting, living alone in my Berkeley apartment. But, we were no longer in Berkeley, and some of my expectations for married life collided head on with the Chilean reality to which Santiago was accustomed. When newly married, I trusted that each day, not long after arriving home from my teaching job, Santiago would follow. We'd spend the evening hours together. My father was my model. Wasn't that what most husbands and dads did? Not in Santiago, Chile. The pressures of work in the big city made for a long day. On most nights Santiago turned the key in the door as the clock struck nine. Those were long, lonely hours.

Busy in my multiple roles of wife, mother and student, I struggled with prickly issues of self-esteem, writing in my journal: "This year I want to make some personal changes. I want to work towards becoming the ideal woman that I've envisioned for years that I'd like to be." The next day I wrote: "I doubt myself so much . . .. Am I selfish?"

Both Santiago and I were perfectionists. I strove to find personal fulfillment as a woman and still live up to his expectations and priorities, which did not always coincide with mine. His voice joined my other inner censors, as I rushed each evening to have everything in order before he arrived: shutters closed, dinner ready, Danny settled, no unnecessary lights burning.

When I was a child, my family didn't touch the painful, the disappointments. My parents argued and my father drank. I watched, listened and suffered anxiety attacks in the bathroom in the night, though I was too young to recognize them for what they were. Afraid of raised voices, angry faces and my mother's crying, I kept silent. If I didn't rock the boat, maybe calm would return. In my weekly letters home, I didn't speak of the ups and downs of married life. I'd already caused my parents enough pain.

I brought my patterns of avoidance to our marriage. It felt safer keeping things to myself rather than facing an unpleasant discussion. So many words left unspoken. Santiago and I struggled to come to grips with our differences of opinion and expectations on the details of daily life. We came to realize that we had different outlooks on life and people. I assumed that most people were well intentioned; Santiago was less trusting. We were also far apart on the political spectrum. Either way — silences or argument — little was resolved. Spats, even major arguments, could start off with a simple misunderstanding of language: the nuances of meaning of a word like "disappointed," or the difficulty expressing and understanding the subtleties of feelings. My pent up emotions became a breeding ground for anxiety. I turned to my journal, and later to a therapist, to develop greater awareness of my emotional needs. But Santiago and I cared about each other, and after a day or two of a mutual silent treatment, we'd make up and focus on the pressing tasks at hand: our child, our jobs, the house.

Although I grew up on another continent, my upbringing had much in common with my generation of Chilean women: the traditional female role and gender values taught in Catholic schools and reinforced in our societies. My mother was an emancipated woman for her generation, a woman of strong beliefs. But her domineering character, along with my parochial schooling, did their job. My self-assertiveness skills were slow to develop. My years in Berkeley liberated me somewhat from those early confines, but, when I married, women's lib was still just a notion in my head. How in this conservative land was I to exercise the feminine freedoms I felt entitled to? With little support and no local role models in those years, I lacked courage and the strength of my convictions. Even in my gringa network we seldom shared intimate marital confidences. It has taken years of introspection, of mistakes made and analyzed and of increasingly honest, open talk with now more liberalized Chilean women to gather the wisdom and courage to put those ideals into practice in my life.

And I'm still learning.

I established a routine of visiting my parents every two years. Missed hugs, kisses and bedtime stories filled each time capsule visit, squeezing the most out of every moment. On one such trip, I told my parents that I suspected I was pregnant.

"Well, you're going to have your hands full," my father answered. In spite of his standard subdued response, I knew he was pleased. As our stay drew to a close, a now familiar phantasmal presence haunted us — the dread of departure and of another long separation.

Back in Chile, the vividness of my parents' faces and voices faded with time. Yet, months after returning, I wrote in my journal: "Pictures of California flash through my mind during the day."

Nicolas was born towards the end of my last semester at the university. I'd been doing extra hours of practice teaching to compensate for the time I'd miss after his birth. I still had to finish my final written thesis. An unfamiliar, frightening specter arrived to torment my nights — insomnia. I listened for Nico's cries and whimpers and, after feeding him, sleep evaded me. I lay awake in a state of anxiety. When I heard the birds begin their morning concert, I accepted defeat. Sleep deprived, I struggled through to the end of the semester, until one day my world imploded. Santiago asked his mother to come over to keep me company. I couldn't bear to be alone. One evening he came home to find me crying uncontrollably.

"Is it something I've done?" he asked.

I shook my head. "No. Yes. I don't know. It's *everything*," I sobbed. "I need you to be more supportive. I want to sleep."

A friend recommended a psychiatrist who came to the house that night. His diagnosis: post-partum depression. We hired a good-natured woman to help care for Nico so I could get some sleep. She seemed an angel to me, someone to lean on and share what felt like the overwhelming responsibility of an infant child. On medication, I slowly crawled out of my dark abyss. With the summer to recuperate, I began to enjoy my new son, and in the fall was able to finish my thesis and start private tutoring. I was beginning to feel normal once more.

While battling my depression, I finally consented to hire our first live-in maid, Rosa. Having a live-in was a foreign experience to me. As *dueña de casa*, I was expected to search for, interview, train and supervise her. Thus began my long, continuing education on how to coexist with domestic help. I cringe thinking of the many mistakes and hurt feelings I produced in this learning process. My first training school was observing how Chilean women handled their domestic help. They warned: maids are sneaky and unreliable; if something is missing or broken, it was the maid; don't be too soft on them.

From the start, I hated the invasion of my privacy. I wanted to raid the refrigerator without being asked: "What do you want, *Señora*?" Maid management didn't come easily — how to give instructions with firmness and kindness and explain how I wanted the housework done. "Rosa, you don't need to take all the sheets and blankets off the bed and remake it everyday," or "Would you please not move the furniture around and vacuum on Saturdays?" I realized I was to provide companionship as well. She had no one to talk to during the day but me.

I was slow in realizing that too much was expected of Rosa. Finally, I insisted to Santiago that she have every Sunday off plus one weekday, defying custom and law permitting a minimum of two Sundays off per month.

I wanted to instill in my boys the values of cooperation and shared responsibilities with which I'd been raised, but my lessons were not reflected in the reality around us. I had clear that our maid was to take care of the house and I would raise our boys. Hah! I just said I would raise the kids, not we. How easy to slip into that lingering mentality — men were the breadwinners and women reared the children. From the time they were small, I expected the boys to clean up their own rooms, instructing Rosa, "Do not pick up after them." Yet, on Rosa's day off, I often found myself alone in the kitchen, hands immersed in dishwater, while Santiago watched a soccer match on television. I'd have to teach cooperation to my husband as well as to our boys.

That summer, five months after Nicolas was born, the two-year cycle of our journeys north was broken. My mother agreed to visit us, a treat after the previous dark months. For the first time since our wedding six years earlier, my mother experienced my Chilean days.

My initial task was to teach her how to get a decent shower. I pointed to the contraption fixed to our bathroom wall. "It's our hot water heater, called a *calefont*," I told her. "To get a consistently hot shower you've got to fine-tune the hot water knob and use equal precision when turning on the cold. It's a delicate balance." I turned on the hot water and, then, the cold. "See? Too much cold water shuts off the hot. Then you quickly turn off the cold and turn up the hot. You'll shiver for several minutes until the water heats up again. Just be glad it's summer."

In the morning she awoke to cries and whistles coming from our parade of street vendors. First came the milkman pushing his little cart stocked with milk, yoghurt, butter and cheese. Then followed by the bread man. We bought some of his freshly baked, crunchy *marraquetas*. He lifted them out of a large box mounted on the handlebars of his homemade tricycle, made of two front wheels, a seat, and a single back wheel. Later the bottle man peddled by, whistling, and I ran out to hand him a bag of empty bottles in exchange for a few coins.

"Maybe tomorrow the broom man will come by," I told her. "You'll know it's him when you hear him call out '*Escoooooobas*' in a gravelly voice. He'll have a clutch of hand-made brooms and feather dusters slung over his shoulder."

Mother accompanied me on my routines around the *barrio*, stopping at the corner *verdulería* to buy chard and squash. On Thursdays we went to the farmer's market where I asserted my right to pick out my own peaches and apricots and haggled over prices.

We visited the coast and then headed in our Kleinbus toward southern Chile, where we met up with Isabel and Gustavo — now reunited — and Isabelita and a girlfriend. It was a Chilean family-style vacation.

We'd been lent a cabin, sight unseen. I'd say this about it — it was free, and did have a view of the lake, but no refrigerator. There was a wood-burning stove to heat our food and water for our showers. My mother and I shared a room along with Nico who barely fit in his *moisés*, his portable, basket-size crib. The wood frame of my bed was broken in the middle, giving it a v-shape. Down from the cabin, mud flats visited by stray cows stood in for a beach. I saw my mother outside, staring out at the lake, and walked up to her. Her eyes were moist. No need to ask her; I could read her mind. *My daughter living in these conditions.*

Mother was a polite, appreciative tourist, and didn't complain other than looking askance at the unrefrigerated soup pot sitting on the wood stove all day. Her Spanish classes at her local community college served her well, but I knew the tremendous effort she was making to understand the family chatter. Most important to her was the time she had with me and her grandchildren.

Before leaving, she said, "You know, I can't help being envious of Señora Olga, living so close to you."

I knew of no words to console her.

Bird Spotting

I walk along the sidewalk bordering the beach. An orange late afternoon sun shimmers over the horizon. The water swirls in and then recedes through mollusk-covered rocks. I stop. There, poised motionless, stands a night heron, its eyes fixed on the shallow water at its feet. I know that its Spanish name is *huairavo*.

From the parking lot behind me come two attendants, a man and a woman, clad in their identifying grimy orange smocks. They want to know what has caught my attention.

"It's a hairavo."

"I call it *pájaro feo*," says the woman.

"Ugly bird? But it's beautiful," I say. "Look how well camouflaged it is among the rocks. It has a long neck but it's tucked in now."

"Huai-ra." The other attendant tries the word on his tongue. Squinting dark eyes, set in a sun-baked face, peer out from under his black cap. He shuffles up beside me for a closer look, his shoes scuffed and worn.

"Huai-ra-vo," I repeat for him.

Just then, quick as a lance, the bird's long neck flashes out and its needle-like beak strikes the water.

"See," I say, "how it catches its dinner!"

"How do you know so much about birds?" asks the woman. Stiff clumps of grey hair poke out from under her cap. Yellow socks sag at her thin ankles.

"I've learned by observing and reading about them."

The man says, "You must read a lot. I like to read, too."

I am about to tell him about the bird guides available in book stores, but I stop. Books are expensive here.

Together we stand there watching the bird for a while.

Then I smile and say, "*Hasta luego.*"

Walking away, I hear the man's voice repeating behind me: "Huai-ra-vo. Huai-ra-vo."

SUZANNE ADAM

5

Marrying Santiago

Conviviendo con Santiago

As a child, I longed for a brother or a sister. I prayed for one, but never mentioned my wish to my parents. Years later I learned from my friend Paula that my mother confided to Paula's mother that she was unable to have more children.

Everyone I knew had sisters or brothers, whose friends would hang out at their houses. Our house was usually quiet, the only voices coming from the radio, the TV, telephone conversations or my parents' frequent bickering. Maybe I wouldn't have been such an anxious child if I'd had someone to talk to when my father's eyes glazed over and his speech turned thick, when the arguments turned violent, when I heard my mother crying in her bedroom in the night. In my childhood daydreams I pictured my grownup self as part of a large, boisterous family, the kind of family I'd read about in *Faith of Our Fathers* textbooks at St. Anselm's and in *The Five Little Peppers and How They Grew*.

I got my wish, but not in the way I imagined.

On a hot summer Christmas Eve, during my first visit to Chile, Santiago and I walked the half block to his brother Roberto's small, attached house. A drooping, Charlie Brown pine branch stood in for a tree next to a crèche lit up in the fireplace. The living room filled with arriving families, depositing piles of packages by the Nativity scene. The noise level grew rapidly, wrapping paper and ribbons flying as the children, my future nieces and nephews, tore open packages. Everyone talked at once. Someone shouted across the room, "Did you give me this?" Little Roberto tried out his new set of drums in the middle of the living room. Definitely not a "silent night." No one knew who gave what. But, once it was revealed, a child's sticky kiss was bestowed in thanks.

It took me years to become accustomed to those Christmas celebrations, so unlike my childhood Christmases when gifts, wrapped like works of art with matching paper, ribbon and cards, were opened slowly, with care. Grandma and Grandpa, Mother and Daddy, Aunt Ida, Aunt Anne — we all watched with polite attention as we took turns opening our gifts.

Marrying Santiago came with extras. Suddenly acquiring three sisters-in-law, a brother-in-law, nieces, nephews and count-less cousins added multiple dimensions to my life. This was the closest I'd get to being a sister and an aunt.

Family events — birthdays, christenings, funerals and wed-dings — filled our year's calendar. Santiago's nephew, José Tomás, was the first of the younger generation to marry. The wedding was the occasion for excitement and preparations that built for months. As was the custom, prior to the church wedding, he and Loreto, his fiancée, were to be married in a civil ceremony held at her home, followed by a small reception. This was the first encounter of the bride's and groom's extended families. Early in the evening, the bride's relatives hovered together in the living room, while we, the groom's family, gathered shyly in the garden, each group sneaking glances, sizing each other up through the wide living room windows. Following the ceremony, and a few glasses of champagne and *pisco* sours later, we began to mingle. The babble grew louder.

"Oh! You're the pediatrician who used to treat my friend Carlos' kids!"

"You were in law school at the Universidad de Chile in 1967? I was the secretary in the office then. I remember you!"

Loreto's father came up to me. "I hear you're a friend of Cindy Alvarez. I ride motor cross with her husband, Roberto." Even I had a connection.

Some weeks later, at the reception following the religious ceremony, amidst hundreds of chattering guests, I smiled, listened and watched people encountering acquaintances of acquaintances, exclaiming: "*Qué chico el mundo!*" "What a small world!" I was an observer, a fly on the wall. It would be decades before I'd feel a part of their small world.

Being the gringa daughter- and sister-in-law had its advantages. They expected me to be different. They were patient and forgiving of my errors in Spanish and my social faux pas. If someone had a problem with me, they were too polite to tell me, but they'd blow off steam about each other to me. I'd listen sympathetically, careful not to take sides. Once again two sisters were not on speaking terms, but that could change anytime. Sibling tensions saddened me, but I didn't suffer over the spats like I did over those in my own family.

Newly married, Santiago and I spent our first weekend escape with one of his cousins, his wife and four small children at their home in Viña del Mar on the coast. Early in the morning children's voices woke us, whining for the maid to bring their milk. Later, while the family conversed for hours over a long lunch, I gazed out the window at the ocean, yearning to take a walk along the beach. Being part of Santiago's family often meant sharing vacation accommodations, definitely handy when the budget was tight. We went where we had an invitation or the opportunity to share. Those occasions required relinquishing some of my American individualism, some of my private self. No romantic weekends for two. A disappointment I had to learn to live with.

One March, with the expensive peak summer vacation season over, we rented a neighbor's small house in the coastal town of Cachagua, which had a long beach, ideal for walking, and a path along the shoreline where we could spot sea otters. Santiago went out running and I walked with the boys. Nico at a year-and-a half still fit into a carrier on my back. I was feeling overweight and Santiago suggested I run. I'd never jogged before, and the country road bordering the coast seemed like the perfect place to start, but after a few runs, I began to feel pain in my lower back. Maybe it was the unfamiliar bed or my walks carrying Nico. I kept running. When we returned home, the pain persisted and I consulted a doctor.

"Stand on your toes and walk," he said. My right foot buckled under me. "I want you to get some tests done. It looks like a herniated disc."

It was.

The doctor ordered me to stay in bed for a month and hope the hernia would return to its proper place.

Stay in bed for a month — with two young children? Thankfully, we had Rosa with us. At the end of a month with no improvement, the doctor said, "You have two choices: live with it, never picking up your children again, or have surgery." We scheduled surgery.

Afterwards, I faithfully performed the exercises a physical therapist taught me and, the following year, I was well enough to travel with Santiago and the boys to California, where we met my parents in Los Angeles. After the obligatory Disneyland visit, we drove winding Highway 1 to San Francisco, where I introduced my boys to beloved landscapes: San Juan Bautista Mission, the steep wooded hills of Big Sur, the Santa Cruz boardwalk, familiar bays and beaches.

This was the first time my father met his second grandchild, now two years old. Again, multiple photo sessions: Nico splashing in the wading pool, lounging in his grandfather's leather armchair, wearing a San Francisco Giants' baseball cap. My father's eyes shone with adoration for his grandsons. How could he resist coming to see them in Chile?

The boys played and ran where I roamed as a child: the surrounding grassy hills, the creek by the house, and the trail around Phoenix Lake. One day Nico came charging down steep Knoll Road, excited and scared. He'd come face to face with a large, antlered buck, a new experience for my city-raised son. This was the start of the boys' immersion into American culture: fishing with Grandpa, using English swear words, eating Big Macs, going to Giants' baseball games, roasting marshmallows and barbecuing at the park. That memorable summer Santiago ran the San Francisco Marathon, the first of many.

Back in Santiago, I felt trapped by my surroundings. I longed to escape the smog and confining city walls and missed contact with the natural world, seldom getting out of the city until summer vacation. Santiago's workload as an appraiser and technical inspector for bank-financed constructions allowed him little free time, while his weekend jogging and cycling routines were sacrosanct. With two small boys, I had plenty to occupy my time, but I missed adult companionship during the evenings and weekends. I sometimes resented that Santiago had opportunities to enjoy the out-of-doors, which I so sorely missed.

Nothing qualified me to be the wife of an athlete. As a single, young woman, I had dabbled in a few sports. I had an acceptable swim stroke, could return a tennis ball and I biked around the streets of Berkeley on my blue Raleigh. My love of the out-of-doors drew me to the trails of California's hills and mountains, where I developed into an avid bird watcher. Hiking, bird watching, camping alongside a mountain stream — those I could get excited about. But competitive sports? I used the unread sports pages of the newspaper to line my garbage can. Track and field? Competitive cycling? I hadn't a clue.

Santiago's rigid training schedule was frustrating in that it severely limited family activities. But I soon learned: once an athlete, always an athlete. It was in his genes. I was unaware at first how this would shape our lives. Danny was just a babe in arms when I took him to the *Estadio Nacional* to watch his father compete in the South American Games, Santiago's last competition running the 400-meter hurdles. I cheered and applauded when he stepped onto the podium to receive his bronze medal. Years later I would watch my sons step onto the same podium.

Santiago often trained on weekends at his sports club, not far from our house, and I'd tag along, letting the boys run around the cross country track. Early on, running flowed in their veins; but now, after my surgery, it was off-limits for me.

When he ceased competitive running, Santiago began cycling and had a hand in founding a cycling club. They arranged occasional rides outside the city and, at first, I'd drive behind them, meeting up with the group for lunch. Why didn't I cycle with him? Their rides were too strenuous and competitive for my tastes and skills. Fueled on high-octane adrenalin, they pedaled hard, eyes on the road, while the landscape — which is what interested me — whisked by in a blur. Driving for hours behind a gaggle of cyclists lost its appeal after several outings, and I often chose to stay home with my boys.

Late one morning, when Santiago was out with the group, I received a phone call from one of the cyclists.

"Susan, Santiago is fine. He's just had a fall." ("Susan" was easier than "Suzanne" for Spanish-speakers.)

"What do you mean that 'he's fine'? Where is he?"

"We're at the hospital." My gut muscles clenched. "He's had a concussion, but is awake and one of the cyclists, a doctor, is making sure he gets good attention."

I wanted to go to him, but the hospital was in an unfamiliar neighborhood. I was anxious and didn't trust myself to find my way. Someone came to pick me up. I found Santiago in a hospital corridor lying on a gurney, his hair matted with blood, but he was conscious and talking. He smiled weakly and reassured me he was okay. He spent several days in the hospital, followed by weeks of bed rest.

Other falls and accidents — a broken collar bone, scrapes and bruises — convinced me that running was definitely safer than cycling.

Other occasional opportunities to get out of the city came up.

One weekend, Isabel lent us her apartment at the coast. Gazing out the car window as we drove there, I thought: *How ironic. California poppies growing unabashedly along the roadside and lining railroad beds, as if they belonged here.*

It's said that the seeds arrived as stowaways in wooden railroad ties shipped from California in the 1800s. And, if I had gotten out and climbed the brown hills whisking by, I'd have heard in the brush that familiar "uh-uh-uh" of the introduced California quail that roam central Chile's hills and valleys. I thought of Chile as an upside-down California — dry in the north and wet in the south. Length- and latitude-wise, California would fit right in the center of Chile.

The briny breezes and the lapping waves of the Pacific on these southern shores invigorated and soothed me. I had always lived within a short distance of the ocean, and I missed it. Funny, gawky, gray and white pelicans cruised along the coastline and squawking seagulls scrambled for scraps discarded by local fishermen as they cleaned the day's catch alongside their red and yellow boats. Shore birds scurried in the ebb and flow, and I wondered if those speckled sanderlings and the Baird's sandpipers stopped to feed and rest on California's shores in their southern migration. I sensed a connection. Those feathered soul mates, like I, considered two continents their home.

Looking out over the Pacific's heaving, shimmering expanse, I felt suspended, between two countries, two homes and two lives. I longed to call a truce to this north-south tug-of-war.

Months later, cheered by the arrival of spring and its welcome wind that swept the skies clear of the suffocating smog, we began to make summer plans. A friend of Santiago's invited us to spend some days in the southern lake region on the island of Fresia in Lake Puyehue, owned by friends who were European immigrants. A purring launch carried us across the teal waters where ahead on a green slope we sighted two unpainted clapboard houses.

Señora Liese showed us to our room that held two beds covered with white, hand-sewn goose down quilts. Wood was the protagonist throughout — floors, walls, beds, chairs, tables, bookshelves, even the shower stalls — all hand-crafted. On a windowsill stood a small vase of wild flowers. I felt transported back to the pioneer days of the 1930s when immigrants, like Liese, settled in southern Chile.

At mealtime, we sat at a long, hand-hewn wooden table, partaking of home-cooked dishes — jams, butter, fresh bread, lamb stew and potatoes — all produced on the island. The next day we followed the steep path leading to the peak, a traditional island hike. In places overgrown with grass and wild bamboo, we lost our way, making our own trail, bending the tall stalks with our feet. Thick forests of laurel, arrayan and wild fuchsia alternated with open meadows, alive with small orange butterflies. Here Santiago and I deepened our love for this region of temperate rain forests, lakes and rushing rivers, where opportunities for fishing, bird watching and hiking abounded. The south drew us like a magnet.

Two years later, Santiago and five friends, former college classmates, learned about a piece of lakeside property for sale near the small *pueblo* of Llifén on Lake Ranco's eastern shore, about 600 miles south of Santiago. Enthused, they flew in a friend's private plane to visit the property. It was love at first sight. Within weeks we were part owners of a piece of what sounded like paradise. It had just one house plus the caretaker's home, but there was enough space, they said, for all of us to build our own cabins. Each family signed up for a two-week period of time that summer.

Our turn came up in late January, and we headed south with the boys in the VW camper loaded with bedding, towels, a new metal chimney for the kitchen's wood stove, fishing equipment, cameras, binoculars and jigsaw puzzles and Chinese checkers for rainy days. We followed the Pan American Highway, *Ruta 5 Sur* — a squiggly, long red line on the map — the artery that joins Chile for 1800 miles, two-thirds the length of the country.

The jagged line of ridges and peaks of the Andes was our constant companion on our left as we headed south through the Central Valley. To the right, the softer contours of the coastal range marked the valley's western limits. It was midsummer and the grass was brown. We passed fields of ripening corn and tidy rows of grape vines spread over gentle slopes. From my map and the road signs I read aloud the names of rivers (I love the sound of the Tinguiririca) and the towns: Peor Es Nada (Better Than Nothing), Chimbarrongo, Entrepiernas (Between Legs), Yerbas Buenas, Villa Alegre, Sal Si Puedes (Leave if You Can). And echoes of past journeys through California: San Rafael, San Clemente, San Carlos, Santa Clara.

"The map reads like a litany of saints." I was Santiago's tour guide; he was seeing his country filtered through my gringa lens.

"Damned truck," he replied. We'd been tailing a cantaloupe-laden, lopsided truck for the past ten minutes. "Can't that pokey fool of a farmer see the line of cars behind him?"

At a clear, straight stretch, he accelerated, while I pressed my feet down on the floorboard.

We played travel games. When we tired of twenty questions, there was a game invented by the boys, "Guess the billboard from the backside." My own backside was crying out for a change of position.

"I have to pee."

"Let's look for a gas station"

"Danny hit me."

The few and far between gas station/rest stops were hot, grimy and fly-ridden. I asked the attendant for the key to the bathroom. The floor was wet, no toilet paper, and a trickle of water dripped into a rust-stained sink.

"Hold your noses," I warned the boys.

Wooden fruit stands lined the roadside offering the season's specialties — corn, tomatoes, melons, peaches, and mounds of watermelons — Pablo Neruda's "green whales of summer." One stand proclaimed itself to be "*El Rey de la Sandia*," The King of Watermelons. We were tempted to stop for a bite to eat at the popular truck stop "*Juan y Medio*," John and a Half. The story was that the owner, Señora Ana, named her restaurant for her husband's well-deserved nickname. Juan measured six feet, four inches tall and weighed in at three hundred pounds. But, to save time and money, we'd brought sandwiches in the cooler. Other roadside restaurants advertised their summer specials on hand-painted signs lined up on fence posts like Burma Shave ads. Read the menu as you drive.

We crossed a bridge, spanning the Biobío River, symbolic of the resistance by the indigenous Mapuche peoples against the Spaniards who called them Araucanos. Past the river, the whitewashed adobe houses and red-tiled roofs gave way to solitary, wooden farmhouses standing in open fields. Like old trees, weathered and gray, they reflected an air of resignation as though they'd given up the fight against the elements in these rainy latitudes. Near the city of Temuco, rolling fields of wheat stretched out on both sides of the road, some tattooed by a harvester with swirling swaths and others, thick with growth, waiting to be cut.

Hours later, we turned left off the Pan American onto a dirt road. I felt like an adventurer, a true trailblazer, as we bounced inland along the twenty-six miles to the town of Futrono. Although accustomed to the dirt roads, part of any travel in Chile, we were heading far from city or highway toward an interior region, where bare, craggy Andean peaks loomed in the east.

Futrono seemed a frontier town with its faded wooden constructions lining the four blocks of the town's center. I stepped into a small grocery store to stock up on provisions. From the store's radio rang out the Bee Gee's singing "Staying Alive." So much for the image of a "frontier town."

We headed the remaining nine miles to the town of Llifén. Before the town, at the deep gorge of the blue-green Caunahue River, we spotted a pair of torrent ducks diving into the white waters.

"Look, boys!" we said. "There. See them? Now watch how they pop up further downstream."

This was what we had come for.

After fifteen hours, we arrived at Llifén, a crossroads town, resting in a narrow valley bounded by high forested cliffs. Leaning, faded wooden houses lined the one unpaved street. A patch of dirt and weeds midpoint where two roads intersected was the closest the town had to a plaza. Two old men sat on a bench in front of a store. A dog of unidentifiable breed chewed at its resident fleas, while local *campesinos* stood about with parcels waiting for the rural bus.

Shortly past the town, we entered the wooden gate that enclosed the house and its grounds. A carpet of delicate, wild grass, dotted with yellow flowers, covered the gentle slopes. The air was a-hum with bees, attracted to the white blossoms of the ulmo tree. The original owner had planted native trees throughout the six acres, enclosing it with a handsome wooden fence. Another fence close to the house kept out the three sheep, our wooly lawn mowers.

The caretaker, Daniel, his wife, Cristina, their three children and their dogs came out to greet us. It was a Hansel and Gretel house: two stories with wide wooden beams outlining the corners, windows and doors. Walking along the path to the house, I saw its sharply sloped shingle roof poking up through the trees, smoke curling out of its chimney. The thick, worn oak door creaked as we entered a tiny, dark hall with a rack for hanging hats and jackets. Another heavy door opened onto the living and dining area, where a faded sofa and wobbly chairs and tables seemed to be waiting patiently for us, the next vacationing family. The red-tiled floor was dark with layers of wax. From the windows I saw trees and fields sloping down to the lake below. The stone fireplace, large enough to hold several people standing, looked to have been transported from some medieval hall. In the small kitchen, Daniel had lit the wood-burning stove, readying it for the evening meal and for warming water for bedtime showers. We hauled our bags up the winding stairs to the second floor whose wood planks had settled at an angle, shaken into this position by the restless volcanic soil.

The caretaker walked us around the property, across meadows of tall grass, up the small hill to a lookout complete with bench, and down the wooden stairs to the beach. He pointed out Señora Neddie's house where we could buy her fresh-baked bread and fruits and veggies from her garden. Further down the road lived Toyita who would make kuchen and empanadas on request.

The next morning the boys took off early with Panchito, the caretaker's son, who showed them the woods with the lianas, long hanging vines, where they played at being little Tarzans. At lunchtime, I stood on the porch and called: "Danny. Nico. Lunch! " A thin voice called back from down at the lake, where they waited patiently on the rocks above a deep, dark pool. Clever trout eluded their lines baited with little live crabs, plucked from under stones. They hunted grasshoppers and, then, with Panchito and his two sisters, organized their own Llifén Song Festival at the bottom of the cracked, empty swimming pool. My boys' summer memories — made in Chile.

Sunday.

We'd stretched out our vacation to the limit and were making the return trip in one day. Heading north, the skies, cleansed by rain, were clear and blue, and the mountain peaks, now on our right, glistened with freshly fallen snow. For a while, four volcanoes were visible within our span of vision. We passed a caravan of pickup trucks — gypsies — loaded high with striped tents and sundry belongings. High on the top of one load sat a little black dog, its fur ruffled in the wind.

Below a bridge, families picnicked and children splashed in the water. I wondered how many rivers we'd cross on our way home, but it was impossible to count all the thin blue lines on the map. How vulnerable Chile was, its geographical unity so dependent upon bridges. Naming rivers and volcanoes, now in the opposite direction, kept us entertained as we headed north.

Hours later, city lights glowed in the distance. Then we were swallowed into the labyrinth of streets and buildings. I began my adjustment, this shift from vegetation to concrete, from the rustle of wind to the roar of traffic. Although home looked good to our road-weary bones, dread lay in my stomach. I had to return to the routines of city life, sharing my space with millions of inhabitants. I'd seek consolation in the images of the tranquil, untamed places we visited, and I'd start planning our next excursion. I thought I heard Patagonia calling.

SUZANNE ADAM

Geography Notes

The news transmitted startling scenes of the Puyehue-Caulle volcanic chain spewing immense, billowing clouds into the sky, showering ash and pumice stone into Argentina.

When the winds changed direction, the ash clouds drifted towards Chile's Lake Puyehue, where authorities were evacuating residents, who resisted leaving their homes and animals.

Months later, invited again to the island house at Puyehue, we find powdery white ash covering every surface while a massive patch of floating volcanic rock spreads over the lake. We venture out in the old launch, opening a path through the thick pumice carpet that tap-taps the sides of our vessel.

We take the seven lakes route. At Lake Panguipulli (Land of the Pumas), the snow-covered Choshuenco volcano pierces the distant skyline. We stop at Vivero Los Boldos, a nursery specializing in native plants. The pastoral scene — grey, clapboard houses under old shade trees, carefully-tended gardens with deep blue hydrangea blooms — is idyllic. Oh, to stay here and work as a gardener's assistant for room and board.

At Conguillio National Park, clouds and sun play tag. Steaming Llaima volcano looms dark and brooding, its snow blackened with soot. The park ranger hands us a map of volcanic risk zones. The road traverses the high risk zone marked in bright red. On the back of the map I read "What to do during an eruption." The last one occurred two years ago this month. We drive across the lava fields, barren grey swaths bereft of all vestiges of forest. But, already, signs of new life: pampa grass and low shrubs. Llaima gives — blocking rivers and forming lakes; and Llaima takes — creating lava deserts around once-forested lagoons.

Here in the deep forest, close to the beginning of all, to the primeval, I am in awe of the magnificent interdependence of all living things. I realize I want my ashes to be scattered onto the earth to become a part of this cycle of birth, death and renewal.

6

Life on a Handkerchief

La Vida en un Pañuelo

En route to a dinner party, Santiago coached me on the names and background of the hosts, a former classmate and his wife, whom I'd met once years earlier. He named others who might be there. It was nine p.m., the usual hour for dinner invitations, though some guests would wander in any time after that.

In the crowded room, humming with chatter, I began the round-robin cheek- kissing and "hola" ritual with the women. Then I encountered a man I thought I hadn't met before, and I was unsure whether to shake his hand or peck him on the cheek. I hesitated, waiting to see if the balding fellow would give me a clue. I was left with my hand suspended in mid-air as he bent to kiss me. Did anyone mention his name?

"Hola."

"Hola." I smiled and pecked the cheeks of two more women as I moved around the room. Then — someone's husband. Kiss or handshake? I developed a simple rule that usually worked: observe what others do and follow suit.

Throughout the greeting ritual, no introductions were made.

Shooting off an urgent plea to the spirit of Sherlock Holmes, I observed the scene, picked up bits of conversation in the buzz, pieced together who was married to whom and their connections with the host and hostess. Seeing my dilemma, Santiago came to my aid, whispering prompts in my ear: "Remember Fernando? You met him at Juan Luis' house that time we went to dinner."

"Santiago," I whispered back, "that must have been at least five years ago."

"You know. He's married to María Eugenia, the sister of Ana María, cousin of my former partner José Antonio."

Most guests seemed to know who I was, so I smiled and acted as though I knew them, and, eventually, I did figure it out.

The only available seat was on the end of the sofa next to the wives of two of Santiago's acquaintances. They were facing each other, forcing me to lean out from the edge of the sofa and strain to be included in the conversation. As they laughed and reminisced about friends and classes, I gathered they went to school together. I envied their shared past and their sense of belonging. I smiled and nodded, but what could I say? I was on the fringe of their conversation, a loose thread in this tightly knit fabric of society.

At eleven o'clock, the hostess called us to the table for dinner. By then, I'd downed a couple of pisco sours, sampled a great variety of hors d'oeuvres and yearned for my bed. When one of the women motioned me to sit next to her, I gladly accepted, doing a rapid mental briefing: *she's Paulina, her husband's Ricardo and they have five children. Right.* I did my best to follow the animated dinner conversation — an apparently funny story about a former classmate. When the maids filed out from the kitchen with several desserts, I abandoned my good intentions and decided to try them all — consolation food to get me through the *sobremesa*, the after-dinner table talk, which would extend into the wee hours. I pulled at my forehead muscles to keep my eyelids up, made a trip to the powder room, and, back in my chair, again attempted to follow the conversation. Desperate, I felt the Restless Leg Syndrome coming on and cast my "let's-go-home" look in Santiago's direction, but he'd gotten a second wind and pretended he didn't see me. He was having a good time, capturing everyone's attention with a favorite anecdote — a long one that I'd already heard. We were among the last to leave — again. At 2 a.m., on our way home, I licked the wounds of my self-esteem and repeated positive affirmations to myself. *I socialize better in small groups. The din of all those voices made it difficult to hear and understand. Shyness isn't a mental disorder. Maybe they didn't know what to say to me either.*

I worried. Was I spending my Chilean life in a bubble, surrounded by cookie-mold people of similar backgrounds? I missed my comfortable California friendships and the rich diversity of people and ideas there. Had my efforts here to fit in stunted my personal growth? Struggling to fit in while being true to myself was a difficult balancing act.

When it was time to consider schools for Danny, Santiago and I agreed that the school should be private. Overcrowded public schools could not provide quality education. We disagreed, however, on the specifics. I wanted my boys to attend an English-speaking school with an international flavor. Santiago argued in favor of the Catholic boys' school where we'd married. Danny's and Nico's cousins were studying there. A Chilean school, he claimed, was more realistic as the boys would be growing up here. *When had that decision been finalized?*

"What about English?" I countered, it being taught just one hour a day at his school of choice. But the school had points in its favor: unlike the English-speaking schools, it was Catholic and in our neighborhood, and it had a strong sports program.

Tradition won out. I finally consented, Santiago agreeing that we'd speak English at home. My mother supplied us with English books for bedtime stories — *Harry the Dirty Dog, There's a Nightmare in My Closet, Curious George* — and the boys picked up both languages with no difficulty, along with a comical sprinkling of Spanglish.

In spite of the school's excellent reputation, the teaching methods — copy from the blackboard and memorize — made my teacher's hair stand on end. Class sizes were large, the classrooms drab and bare, but I had to admit the teachers were dedicated. At parents' meetings, I felt as if I were back at my old school, St. Anselm's, in the 1950s, stifling my rebellious voice within, wanting to protest narrow opinions or propose alternative ideas. But, if I spoke up, all eyes would be on me. In front of groups I was excruciatingly aware of my strongly-accented Spanish and imagined the parents thinking: "Of course she's got these liberal ideas . . . she's a gringa." I didn't want to stand out. Marrying into the *barrio alto* was shaping my path, my friends, my decisions, my life.

An American friend once commented to me, "I have no past before I came to Chile." I knew what she meant. Seldom did anyone show curiosity about my pre-Chile life — my studies, my travels, my work. In this close society of shared school, neighborhood and family connections, I found it difficult to make friends with Chilean women.

I've always felt like family with Santiago's sisters. We call each other on the phone just to talk. My contacts with the wives of Santiago's closest buddies are limited to our activities as couples, an occasional dinner party or a movie. But with none of them did I develop that close woman-to-woman, best friend-who-lends-you-clothes sort of relationship. No phone calls to chat about nothing in particular or a visit over a cappuccino. With no sisters, daughters, girl cousins, or aunts in Chile, I yearned for a greater Chilean female network.

In the early years, I depended upon my English-speaking friends for coffee conversation, other young women married to Chileans. We gravitated towards each other, our shared language, experiences and culture uniting us as we learned our way in this country. We dubbed ourselves the "gringa group." Danny and Nico played with their toddlers while we examined our expatriate lives, complained about Chilean drivers, recommended pediatricians and revealed where to find chocolate chips. But, when Danny started at his all-Chilean school and the children of my American friends entered English-language schools, we had fewer occasions to see each other. My boys formed new friendships at their school and in our neighborhood. At work, I tended to form closer friendships with the English-speaking teachers and watched as good friends moved on. I became aware of how vulnerable my friendships were here, fraught with uncertainty. Will she, too, move away in a year or two?

Pouring over the morning newspaper, Santiago would turn directly to the obituaries, informing me that so-and-so's wife's grandfather died. "Uh-huh," I would mumble as I read editorials and international news before turning to scan the society pages. Maybe, among the photographs of smiling people at business seminars, golf championships, benefit bingos and beach resorts, I'd recognize a name or a face. I continued to be amazed at the many ways this community resembles the intricate weave of fine, old cloth, a bewildering web of intertwining strands of relatives, friends, school buddies, acquaintances, co-workers and colleagues.

Wherever we went, we encountered someone we knew, usually someone Santiago knew, even on a mountain trail in remote Patagonia. Entering a restaurant, I felt the eyes of the diners looking us over, checking us out. Maybe they knew or recognized us from somewhere within this network. When visiting California, I'd catch myself looking around a restaurant or theater for a familiar face. But no longer.

Connecting names with faces within this wide web is an essential social skill — one in which I have always been sorely lacking. If only I'd inherited my father's talent for making friends in new situations and remembering names. Ah, yes, the names. Not just María, but María José, María Teresa, María de Los

Angeles, María Angélica, María Luisa. Juan and José combinations are just as dizzying. When I bumped into the mother of one of Nico's classmates, I couldn't remember if her husband was Juan Pablo or José Pablo. Or was it Juan Antonio?

"Er . . . How's . . . your husband?"

Would I ever keep them all straight? Connect the name with the face? Everyone remembers me and my name. I'm the gringa.

As my boys grew older, connecting names with their friends' faces required a unique set of memory neurons. My consolation was that even Santiago had a problem with this. When new friends came by our house, no names were offered. Clearly, I was the mother. But who were they? It was just "hola" and a peck on the cheek. Not that an introduction helped. They all went by nicknames: Ofo, Tufo, Rata, Negro, Mono, Satanás, Fofito. I couldn't call them these names to their faces, even if I could remember which face went with which name.

One day a young man called on the phone and greeted me with "Hola Tía", aunt. (I'm "aunt" to dozens of young men and women). "Is Nicolás home?"

"Who's calling?" I asked.

"Raimundo."

Now was he el Negro or el Mono? Was he the tall, skinny one with long stringy hair? Or the short, husky fellow with a beard?

"Hola. *Cómo estás?*" I answered. Again, I did a little pretending.

A Johnny-come-lately, I couldn't get it straight — the names, the stories, the connections, the lingo. Everyone was laughing, but the joke had to be explained to me. Would I ever get it?

I've learned to employ every memory strategy within my grasp to remember first names, but then am faced with an additional hurdle — family names. So different from the American melting pot, last names in Chile are the key to just about all social interactions. They define to others who you are, placing you within this network. If you can't keep track of last names, you are sunk.

At a family lunch one day, my sister-in-law's mother-in-law, Doña Meme, was telling a story about a certain José Miguel Larraín. Since there are many Larraín families in Chile, Santiago's mother asked: "Is that the Larraín Valdés or the Larraín Echeñique family?" She had added the mother's maiden name to clearly identify the family in question.

"No, mamá," answered Santiago. "The Larraín Videlas. The ones from La Serena. Remember their daughter María Luisa, married to Juan Jorge Molina, who lived across from us on Suecia Street?"

I half-heartedly attempted to follow the tortuous explanation of the various Larraín families, the town they originally came from, who was dead or living, who married whom and where they went to school. But, somewhere along the way, I lost it. I couldn't take much more. Nobody ever asked if I was from the Adam Cross family, Cross being my mother's maiden name.

My difficulty with names and faces frustrated Santiago. He claimed it was a lack of effort on my part. I protested that my memory wasn't wired in Chile and lacked the necessary pigeon-holes to store this information. In recent years, I think he may have resigned himself to my poor memory.

After I'd been in Chile some years, my mother made a surprising discovery. Her grandmother's brother, Robert, immigrated to Chile from Scotland at the turn of the century and started a store in Valparaiso, Casa Riddell, mentioned in history annals as the store immigrant British ladies frequented. We searched out and met some of his descendants here. I sometimes imagine Great Grand-uncle Robert watching over me as I strive to make a life here. I wonder what life was like for his wife Elizabeth in the Chile of the early 1900s. Did she struggle with the language? Did she ever come to think of this as home? This Chilean connection of mine is the ace up my sleeve when the talk inevitably gets around to names and relations.

When my father-in-law's cousin, Ewan Gordon, passed away, Santiago and I attended the burial service at the Cementerio de los Disidentes, the Dissidents' Cemetery, in Valparaiso. Built on a hilltop overlooking the harbor, it faces the main cemetery across a narrow lane. With the arrival of the early immigrants to the port, many of whom were Protestant, it was decided they could not be interred in the Catholic cemetery, and a separate cemetery was created. As we entered, my eyes scanned the names on the tombstones. The first one I saw read "Adam." I found another one — "Stenhouse," — my Aunt Anne's middle name, and also the last name of Robert's mother, my great-great grandmother. They were all immigrants, their tombstones indicating their place of origin, mainly from Scotland. Someday I'll return to see if Uncle Robert is buried there and explore for more family connections.

Danny's and Nico's legal last names are Gordon Adam — my maiden name tagged onto Santiago's last name. To assist the puzzled office clerk who asked for my complete name, not in her usual repertoire, I told her: "Adam like the chewing gum, but without the final "s," and Cross like the pen." For my married name, I offered, "Gordon like the gin."

With sufficient repetition, I do remember people's names, like those of Santiago's cycling friends. A group recently got together for lunch at the country house of his buddy, Enzo. While some went out cycling, we set a long table with a white cloth in a shady corner of the garden and toted a variety of salads and meats from the kitchen. The cyclists returned with hearty appetites. Table talk was loud and lively with jokes and details of past rides. The strains of an Argentine tango mingled with the din. I sat, drowsily listening to the chatter and the music and inhaling the heady aromas of *tinto*, red wine, and sliced sweet melons on platters. After coffee, some stayed at the table conversing, while I joined the women lying in the grass under the summer sun. We talked about diets, our kids and the latest romance in the cycling club. With the cooling late afternoon wind, we drifted inside the house where the talk continued over tea, toast and cake. I didn't want the day to end, relishing the long, lazy afternoon in the country, that brief escape from city life. Among those old friends, I felt at home.

My father had worn the badge of a San Francisco policeman and his father made his living as a waiter and a bank guard. My maternal grandfather was a typesetter for the *Oakland Tribune*. With that working class background, social standing was not high on my list of priorities, leaving me unprepared for the Chilean reality of marked class differences.

At the university in Berkeley, I was comfortable with my choice to be a "dormy" rather than a sorority pledge, while my Peace Corps experience turned me into an advocate for the poor. I arrived in Chile, I believed, free of prejudices, only to find myself immersed in Chile's upper echelon, which only mixed with GCU, *Gente Como Uno*, people like oneself.

I wanted to kick myself one day when I heard myself asking a woman I'd just met, "Where do your kids go to school?" and, then, "Where do you live?" Her answers would reveal her social status.

Another day self-disgust filled me when, fuming at an aggressive male driver who wouldn't let me change lanes though I'd been signaling for two blocks, I grumbled under my breath, "*roto con plata.*" Low class new-rich. Or the time I mentally cursed a woman driver. "*Vieja cuica.*" Upper class snobby old lady. I'd fallen into the pervasive Chilean habit of sizing up people, assigning them to a class or category by their appearance and other telltale signs. I didn't like this person I'd become.

It didn't take me long to realize that Chileans segregate themselves based on physical appearance and behavior — not so much skin color, but facial features, hair texture, clothes, and, equally important, speech and manners. Other defining factors include neighborhood, school affiliation and last name. Money helps, but is not a strict requirement. Class awareness is as present as the air we breathe.

SUZANNE ADAM

Yet, there is no gigantic glass dome over the barrio alto, separating it from the rest of the city's inhabitants. Sitting behind the wheel at a red light one day, I watched the faces peering out the windows of a smoke-spewing bus roaring past, faces of people going to and from work, people with names, families, stories, hopes and dreams. We mix with each other day after day — supermarket clerks, gas station attendants, government office workers — but we interact superficially, taking little notice of each other. At the end of the day, it's back onto the graffiti-covered buses or the sleek, swooshing subways or the SUVs to one's own sector of town.

Punctually, on the twenty-first of each month the other end of town comes to me — Tito, our window washer. A short, compact Mapuche man, he appears at our front door with his yellow plastic bucket, dishwashing liquid, a squeegee and a rag protruding from his back pocket. The first time he came, I watched him deftly swirl the squeegee back and forth down the window pane lickety-split, wipe it with a rag and move on to the next window. He was quiet and withdrawn. But the next month, when I asked him about his family and his work, his face opened, like a curtain parting, to reveal twinkling eyes and an easy smile. He spoke of his childhood in a small southern town and of his father raising him after his mother left them. With modest pride he related how he managed to finish school and teach himself to type on a used typewriter, later becoming secretary of his church.

Each month I learned more about him. "A cousin sold me a second-hand computer and I've learned to use it. My wife and I play cards at night on the computer."

"Where do you go after here?" I asked. His regular jobs are offices, stores and some private homes.

"No more work today. I've got to go buy a part for my car."

"Your car?" I couldn't disguise my surprise. I knew he traveled by bus to get around to his different jobs.

A big smile spread across his dark round face. "I bought

a little used Subaru. We use it on the weekends to go grocery shopping and visit friends out in the country."

Later, I heard him and Carola, our day maid, in the kitchen chattering like two magpies. He seems centered and contented with his life, and every month I remember to be grateful that he is a part of our lives.

One spring day, I arranged for a bricklayer to come to give me an estimate for a small patio.

He called. "Señora, I'll be there at noon tomorrow."

"Fine," I answered, knowing that "noon" was relative.

Early the next morning he called again. "I'll be there at 10:30."

"OK." That was a surprise — a worker arriving early.

At 10:15 he called from a public phone, traffic noises in the background.

"Señora, my truck's broken down. I won't make it today." No big surprise.

He appeared early the next morning — a large man with graying hair pulled back into a long ponytail. Stretched over his well-nourished belly, his tee shirt proclaimed "American Wilderness."

Noting my accent, he asked me in English, "Do you speak English?"

Now that was a surprise. "Where did you learn English?" I asked.

"I lived eighteen years in Los Angeles, California."

"You're kidding! I'm from California!"

"I was very happy there," he said. "You know, I'd heard a lot about how badly Latinos were treated there, but people were always friendly with me."

He chatted on, answering my questions. The sun was high overhead when I suggested maybe he could take the measurements for my patio. We shook hands as he left. (Never a kiss on the cheek. You greet your doctor with a cheek kiss, but never

SUZANNE ADAM

a worker.) With this touch of hands we confirmed this brief meeting of opposite ends of town. Mr. American Wilderness might have made a good neighbor.

Chileans refer to their slender, geographically-isolated country as an island culture. But, what describes the country best is the oft-repeated saying: Chile *es un pañuelo*, Chile is the size of a handkerchief. You're never far removed from someone who knows someone you know — so you'd better keep the names straight.

Bumblebee

From the window I watch a bumblebee visiting the tiny white veronica blooms in my garden. I smile at its drunken flight pattern. My furry visitor is the non-native *Bombus terrestris* imported from Europe. The population of the native orange and black Chilean bumblebees is in decline. I am on the lookout for a native, although I'm unlikely to find one here in the city.

Welcome
yellow, black-banded thief
robbing perfumed nectar
from my apricot blossoms.
With buzzing industry
you dislodge pale velvet petals
that shower downwards,
spring snowflakes carpeting the grass.

Winged Robin Hood of my backyard forest
take what you may
from these ephemeral bursts.
In summer's awakening
I'll gather golden apricots
sweet surrenders of vanished blooms.

7

Arrivals and Partings

Llegadas y Partidas

One morning I went outside to discover the driver's side of our trusty Fiat propped up on bricks. A *ladrón* had stolen the tires in the night. Having no driveway or garage to pull the car in was a problem. And wouldn't it be nice to have two bathrooms, a larger kitchen and garden, we said?

Moving to California was no longer discussed. Santiago had steady work, and the boys were firmly rooted in this country, with neighborhood and school friends. I began to house hunt, scanning the ads in the newspaper and keeping an eye out for *Se Vende* signs in the area.

A year had passed when one day I invited Danny to go with me to see a place. We both liked it immediately, although it needed some work. It took months for the sale to go through due to complications with a mortgage we'd been unaware of. We lined up workers and put our little house, our abode for the past twelve years, on the market.

Then unexpected news came from up north. My mother convinced my father to take a cruise that would start in Valparaiso, Chile. She had always wanted to travel through the Straits of Magellan, she'd told him. Fifteen years after our wedding my father finally agreed to visit us in Chile. Work on the new house had begun and we would move in before they arrived — we thought. But, the work took longer than planned. Months longer. The house was not ready for my parents' arrival, but we managed, giving our bedroom over to them (as they had done for us), Santiago and me in the boys' beds and the boys in sleeping bags.

My father laughed and played with his grandsons. He said he liked our little house and showed no dismay at the tight quarters, the iffy showers or our lack of a clothes dryer, garbage disposal and dishwasher. You never would have guessed it took him fifteen years to agree to come here.

We took them on the train to the south to stay at the lakeside cabin at Llifén. The lumpy beds and smelly bathrooms on the old train didn't faze him. At the cabin he was relaxed, venturing out to pick blackberries for our dessert and to fish with the boys. He avoided hilly areas, aware of his ever-present angina. Otherwise, he was in fit condition. In the years since I left home, he'd given up all alcohol — thanks to Al-Anon and AA — and smoking and had lost weight. We snapped more photos. He was smiling in every one.

The days flew by and we drove my parents to Valparaiso to board their cruise ship. Again, false cheery good-byes.

In the fall we made the move to our new house and bought a beagle puppy whom we named Max. At first, we were swimming in the house with all that space: three bedrooms, the master bedroom downstairs with its own bathroom, a den, a study, kitchen, separate living and dining room AND a visitor's bathroom, a maid's room and bath. Upstairs a bedroom for each boy, a bathroom, and a storage room we invented in the attic. It took us very little time to fill it. The garden was smaller than I'd wanted, but there was room enough for me to satisfy my need to touch soil and exercise my green thumb. We even had full-grown apricot and lemon trees. Nico insisted on planting his potted foot-high avocado tree which we tucked into a corner of the walled backyard.

In our larger home, Santiago and I began hosting the Gordon family Christmas Eve festivities. The plop of ripe apricots hitting the ground reminded me it was jam-making and Christmas cookie time — right in the hottest days of early summer.

Christmas Eve was a repeat performance of my first Christmas here — but the family had grown. Four generations filled our house, including a couple of boyfriends and girlfriends. One of the teenagers played Santa Claus, wearing my father's old Santa hat and beard. When the last of the family trickled out at 2 a.m., I rushed to fill our four stockings by the fireplace, determined to preserve some of my childhood traditions.

Our backyard became the usual setting for family barbeques, since most of the relatives lived in apartments. The barbeques acquired a routine:

Put out extra plates — for I never know how many will show up (a difficult lesson coming from a family of three, where guests came by confirmed invitation). Pull out every available garden chair and count. Seats for twenty. The doorbell. Sisters- and brothers-in law, cousins, nieces and nephews pour in with platters and bags of food: beef and chicken wings, spicy sausages, *ensalada chilena* of tomatoes and onions, chips, cheeses and chopped green chilies. Wine and pisco. With little planning, there's plenty for all. Some wander into the TV room; men huddle in groups to discuss the woes of the Chilean soccer team; I run in and out with glasses, ice and soda bottles, or join the women at the picnic table to hear tales of kids and a trip to Miami; adults laugh and children shout, running about, upturning rocks to search for sow bugs and for Speedy Gonzalez, our pet tortoise.

Here was the boisterous family of my childhood daydreams.

One evening, after the last guest left, Santiago and I were

in the kitchen cleaning up. Suddenly, he put his arms around me and buried his face in my neck, sobbing. Alarmed, I asked, "What's the matter?"

He whispered into my neck, "Thank you for leaving your country and your family and for getting all my family together."

I didn't know what to say, pleased, yet saddened to be reminded of my losses. We stood holding each other.

Two years after my parents' visit, my mother wrote that my father was undergoing a series of tests due to pain in his legs. Months later came the doctor's diagnosis: Lou Gherig's disease, or amyotrophic lateral sclerosis (ALS). I knew nothing of the disease, but learned that it was progressive. I decided to visit my parents with the two boys at Christmas.

My father had grown thin. He moved about with effort, but the worst was his great difficulty sleeping and swallowing. He'd often get up from his bed at night to sleep in his leather living-room chair in a semi-reclined position, sometimes falling while making his way to the chair. None of us slept well. Though we tried at mealtime to keep up a cheerful conversation, we couldn't escape the excruciating difficulty he had swallowing. The boys pranced around in Santa hats and beards, trying to make him laugh, but in the photos taken then, he was seldom smiling, his eyes dark wells of sadness.

One day I took him out for a ride to China Camp on the bay, a place where he used to fish. "I'm going to kick the bucket before long," he said. I was at a loss for words. Here was my chance to let him talk about his fears, about death, to give voice to all the words we'd never spoken, but I was unable to break through that pattern of avoidance of the uncomfortable. I glossed over his comment with nice words, missing the opportunity he had given me.

Mid-January I had plane reservations for nine year-old Nico and me to return to Chile. Danny, fourteen, stayed on to keep my parents company and to be a support to my mother. It was summer in Chile and he'd return for the start of school in March.

I hugged my father good-bye. "I'll see you soon, Daddy." He nodded his head, managing a weak smile.

We thought this would be a long, drawn-out illness.

Nico and I arrived back to Chile in time to help Santiago celebrate his birthday. The next day my mother called.

"Daddy's in the hospital. They've put him on morphine."

"Call a priest," I said. "I'll get there as soon as I can."

The following day, I was on the plane back to California, praying I'd make it there in time. The journey seemed eternal.

Someone picked me up at the airport — I don't remember who — driving me straight to the hospital. I walked into the room uncertain what I'd find, but saw that my father was still conscious. My mother and I hugged. How wan and tired she looked. I bent over my father and took his hand. "I'm back, Daddy." He smiled. His speech was labored, but he managed to say how proud he was of his family. He had requested no life-prolonging devices and was breathing with great difficulty. My mother and I took turns at his bedside. During the day, Danny was attending the local middle school, where he had hippie-offspring classmates with names like Sequoia and Larkspur. The next afternoon I called my mother who had been resting at home. "I think you'd better come now." Soon after she arrived, my father's breathing became slower and more labored, until, finally, he let go.

Opening my eyes to the January darkness the next day, I remembered I was in my childhood bedroom and that my father was gone. Something had woken me. I sniffed, inhaling a repulsive odor. The dawn silence was punctuated by growling, scuffling noises coming from the basement. Groping for the light switch, I checked the clock. Six a.m. I poked my head into my mother's bedroom.

"Mom, what's that awful smell?"

"I think they're skunks."

The stench seeped through the heating vents, enveloping us like a smothering blanket. I thought of the Bhopal tragedy in India, and considered the possibility we were being gassed.

Danny stumbled in. "Mommy, what's that smell?"

"Skunks," I sighed.

The three of us spread out like a SWAT team throwing open all the windows in the house, leaning out for gulps of uncontaminated air. Then we huddled in the kitchen to discuss a plan of action, but options were depressingly limited. It was Sunday. Not just any Sunday, but Super Bowl Sunday, and the San Francisco Forty-Niners, the local team, were playing. My father's dying wish had been to live to see the Super Bowl.

I yanked out the phone book and scanned the emergency numbers. Maybe the fire department? The operator on duty suggested the sheriff's department, which referred me to the Humane Society. Finally, a kindly soul gave me a name and a telephone number.

His phone rang. Please pick up the telephone. Please.

"Hello?" A man's voice.

"Is this Jack? Can you help us?" I explained our dilemma.

"Yeah, I'll be glad to come over — after the game."

My heart sank. The game wouldn't end until late afternoon. We'd have to spend the entire day bundled in jackets with the smelly critters cavorting beneath us. It was impossible to think about eating there. We dressed and escaped to Hilda's Coffee Shop for breakfast, basking in the warmth and the appetizing odors of hot coffee, toast, bacon and eggs.

On the way home, we stopped at the market to buy more Glade. The canisters lined up on the shelf held promising titles. With Sea Mist and Mountain Breeze in hand, we headed back to the crime scene.

We sprayed with a vengeance, but our exorcisms were no match for the odor. It was man-made Glade versus nature's own Skunk Mist. There was no escaping the stench. It hung with the clothes in the closets, hovered in the car and clung to the insides of our nostrils.

In the late afternoon, a young man drove up in a Volkswagen Beetle. He introduced himself and handed me his card. Jack Black. Skunk Buster.

"How did you get into this business?" I asked.

"I'm a policeman and do this during my off-duty hours. There's an amazing demand — raccoons in chimneys, squirrel nests in attics, skunks in basements . . .."

In my naiveté, I assumed he'd escort the skunks from underneath our house immediately, leading them away like a Pied Piper. We listened in disbelief while he explained how we were to set up the trap.

"Look." He lifted the door of the cage-like trap. "Just put an open can of cat food in here. The skunk goes in; the door closes. When you've got one, call me."

"But my father's memorial service is Tuesday," I said. "Family and friends are coming to the house for a buffet afterwards."

He shrugged his shoulders. "There's no other way."

Danny gamely accepted the position of official trap setter, placing the contraption in the back patio. As dark descended, we took turns tiptoeing by the window to see if we had any takers.

"Nothing yet," I called.

We prepared dinner.

Danny made another pass by. "Still nothing."

Half an hour later. "Bingo!" Danny cried. "There's something in the cage!"

My mother and I rushed to the window. Two small, beady eyes peered at us in the dark from behind its prison bars. The three of us stared back.

One down, but how many to go? That was the mating season for these mustelids, the Skunk Buster explained, and there were probably several male skunks under our house, competing for a female. Employing their musky attractions was part of the mating game.

"What if they do it again tonight?" My mother voiced the fear we all harbored.

"We'll just have to spray more Glade and explain the situation," I said, hoping the house wouldn't smell like a disinfected bathroom.

Early the next morning, we called the Skunk Buster. "We've got one."

When he arrived, he climbed into heavy, plumber-like overalls and donned a gas mask, cap and gloves.

"What are you going to do?" I asked.

"Chloroform it."

"Do you have to?"

He clearly cared for wildlife, but explained that this was the only realistic solution. It was either them or us. The skunk's finale saddened us. Another death was not what we expected.

Already I was missing my father. I touched his empty leather chair where he watched football games on television and took his afternoon siestas. I'd miss his sense of humor. Once, while I was at Girl Scout Camp, I received a typewritten letter from an alleged prison inmate, claiming he wanted to meet me. An unsavory mug shot was attached. Since my father worked in law enforcement, I recognized the secret hand behind the letter. Now as I look at photos of my father before he became ill, he always seemed to be caught in gales of laughter

That night, the eve of the memorial service, the skunks considerately took the night off. By morning, the smell had downgraded from nauseating to unpleasant. Another round of Glade and we prepared to receive our visitors.

"Sorry for the smell," we said, "Skunks in the basement."

We told the details of our ordeal and of the Skunk Buster's visit. Ripples of laughter spread among the friends and family gathered with us. They reminisced about my father's great sense of humor. Then the gregarious voice of old friend Mary captured everyone's attention. "I remember once I complained to Tony about having only one bathroom in our house." She paused for dramatic effect. "The next day a Port-a-let appeared on our front lawn."

Yes, everyone agreed, Tony delighted in playing the occasional practical joke. And now that he'd missed the Super Bowl, he'd found other entertainment.

Fall

A morning walk. The fall leaves display such variation of colors. The oblong chestnut leaves wear a brown lace trim. Blotches of brown and yellow have invaded the oak leaves. The ornamental cherry leaves drift to the ground, faithful to their burgundy hue, while claret seeps into the greens of the maple. The ground below one tree is circled with a thick skirt of yellow leaves as if they agreed to leap off their branches together, lemming-like.

I spot a bright yellow butterfly in the neighborhood and check my field guide. Looks like it's a cloudless sulphur. Nice name. How can I entice it to visit the buddleia in our garden?

I haven't heard the delicate call of the fío-fío, the white-crested eleania, in days. They must have embarked on their long journey. I wonder how they do it. Such fragile creatures can't possibly travel alone. Do they organize themselves by neighborhood? Do they have a meeting spot? According to my notes, this is the longest they've stayed in the city since I've kept record.

Rake and broom days. Below the apricot tree spreads a blanket of lemony-yellow leaves. Our snowball bush is blushing a deep crimson. My feet crunch along the leaf-strewn sidewalks where a city worker sweeps with a large palm frond. The frond clears a broader path than any rake or broom.

I perform a raking operation on my side of the closet, sorting what I no longer use, putting away summer clothes and making space for winter shawls and sweaters, producing in me a feeling of lightness. I avoid looking at Santiago's side of the closet.

The pungent fall fragrances and the soft, buttery sunlight evoke nostalgia in me. Are we expats more prone to this autumn wistfulness?

8

Little Lulu's Club

El Club de las Pequeñas Lulus

"Why can't the maid do it?"

I'd asked Nico to make his bed. It was noon and he'd just emerged from his cocoon. That response was a frequent cop-out not just in our household, but in many Chilean homes where a maid was employed. From my students I heard not, "The dog ate my homework", but rather, "The maid put it somewhere and I couldn't find it." One theory had it that this male attitude towards domestic chores was actually the fault of Chilean mothers who raised their sons to expect to be waited on. A terrible doubt haunted me. Was I guilty of perpetuating the macho syndrome in my own family? Was I part of the vicious circle of mothers, maids and machismo? I needed to give this some serious thought.

One day, when Santiago's mother came for lunch, I complimented her hair. She had made one of her infrequent trips to the neighborhood *peluquería*, but something unusual caught my eye. What was this? Green eye shadow? Other than occasional applications of lipstick, I'd never seen her use any type of makeup. I asked about the eye shadow. She laughed. "I came across it while cleaning a drawer. I'd hidden it away from Roberto — he disapproved of it — and I forgot all about it." Her candor surprised me. Don Roberto had passed away the year before. Was this a small sign of newfound freedom?

But no, like a plump brown hen, except for her snow-white hair, Señora Olga continued to cluck and worry over her brood of five children, eleven grandchildren and growing clutch of great-grandchildren. Her family was her life. I'd never heard her lament unfulfilled dreams or yearn for anything more.

Señora Olga's upbringing was like that of most Chilean women of her generation in society's upper echelons. Born in 1910, she and her sister, Elena, spent their childhood on the family farm, Las Brisas, near the provincial town of Talca. Their mother, Benigna, reportedly a cultured woman who played the piano and had a pleasant singing voice, died when they were teenagers. A central figure in the girls' lives was their nanny, affectionately called *Ñaña*, who had been with the family for years. According to hearsay, their father, Victor, wasn't much into child rearing, spending a good deal of time at the men's club in town. Brought up as befit young ladies in the privileged class of *gente-gente* (decent, educated people like themselves), their formal education did not go beyond the Catholic girls high school they attended. With a maid and Ñaña always present, they had little opportunity to learn domestic skills. They did, however, learn to drive the black 1927 Ford sedan their father bought them, so they could take him into town.

"How did you learn to drive?" I asked her.

She shrugged. "Oh, by reading the manual and practicing on country roads."

After Señora Olga married Roberto, they sold their part of the farm to Elena and her husband, Hector, and moved to the outskirts of Santiago and, later, into the city. She devoted her days to raising their children and making ends meet as the money from the farm sale dwindled. Don Roberto, as I always called him, went from one unprofitable enterprise to another, yet Señora Olga, who had only learned to cook basic dishes for the family, usually managed to have some domestic help. Out of necessity, she learned to sew. Through the years, she meticulously mended and darned all of our family's moth-nibbled sweaters and worn socks — which was a gift as I hated that job. When she came for Sunday lunch, she always offered, "Do you have any mending for me to do?" She wanted to feel useful.

When her children were grown, Señora Olga took a clerical job in a government office, working until retirement. Selfless to the point of being self-effacing, her thoughts were always focused on others' needs. Only in later years did she become needy and dependent, though, with growing stubbornness, she refused to admit it. She continued to provide us with motherly advice. "Bundle up or you'll catch cold" was her favorite.

I asked Santiago if he was expected to help around the house when he was growing up. He said he did have to make his bed and help sweep when they had no maid. Yet, his generation of children was not usually expected to cooperate with domestic chores; nor were the men, for they brought home the money, while the women were there to raise children and supervise the help. Young women were to finish high school, and, perhaps work as a secretary, living at home until they married and began a family. Santiago's sister Isabel told me she wanted to go to college to study history, but, being the eldest, she was needed to help support the family. Santiago was the only family member to get a university education. Tía Elena bore six children, who gave her a total of forty-six grand- and great-grandchildren by the time she died at age ninety-three.

How different were my childhood years in our small family. My father and I were only children, so cousins, aunts and uncles were few. Saturday was housecleaning day, my mother allotting the jobs. My father took out the garbage and did the outside work. I picture him wearing baggy khaki pants, a plaid wool shirt and his San Francisco Giants baseball cap, pushing a wheelbarrow with a load of soil for the garden. My mother and I took care of the dusting and vacuuming. We three were a team. I learned to mop floors, cook tuna casserole, make a dress from a McCall's pattern, bathe the dog and trim suckers from the rose bushes. It was in that household that my concept of mothers evolved. My mother's background and experiences — university graduate, dedicated professional, perfectionist homemaker and overachiever — contrasted vividly with those of Santiago's mother — submissive wife raised in traditional country mentality, conformist to rigid social expectations and not curious about the world beyond her limited borders. I never judged them on these differences; they were raised in dissimilar societies where opportunities and expectations for women varied.

Chile's maze of mother, maid and macho traditions caught me unprepared. After Rosa left us, a colorful, diverse parade of maids filed through our home over the years: caring, competent, grouchy, and bossy (we called her "The Sergeant"). Two got pregnant; one's boyfriend was a terrorist. Another had a knack for breaking kitchen glasses and burying the evidence in the garden. Clementina, "The Mumbler," scurried about the house talking to herself, eyes lowered, insisting on mopping the kitchen floor twice daily. Veronica, the last of our live-in maids, was *buena como el pan*, "as good as bread." I enjoyed talking with her. She was practical, down-to-earth and funny, and shared with me a love of the outdoors. Her domestic practices perplexed at times. To rid our electric coffee maker of ants she cleaned it with Clorox, resulting in a shocking brew the next day. Brown shoe polish was her solution to cover the evidence when she over-zealously polished the varnish off Aunty Belle's antique rocking chair. How we laughed when she discovered she'd stored the laundry detergent in the refrigerator.

The topic of maids slipped into the girl talk at every lunch, dinner and tea time I attended.

"Have you found a good nanny for your baby?"

"My nanny's going home to care for her aging mother; does anyone know of someone to replace her?"

"Our maid is an excellent cook, but I've noticed small things missing lately, yet I have no proof . . .."

It was difficult to live with them and harder without them. My life would have been completely different without María, Rosa, Carmen, Veronica, Carola and all the others who gave me the gift of time — time to pursue my career, studies, sports and simply to put my feet up after a day of teaching.

As the boys grew older, I insisted they help out, especially on the maid's days off. Soon Santiago got the message. We began taking turns in the kitchen cleanup brigade on weekends. In the absence of the boys, Santiago became my official weekend dishwasher. But with a maid in the house most of the time, it was an upstream battle. Looking back, some of my lessons seemed to have stuck. But, lord, it took a long time.

With our boys becoming more independent, evenings were often just the two of us. When Santiago called at nine p.m. to say he was staying at his sports club for dinner, I did not leap for joy. I'd been waiting for him, the fish in the oven overcooked. I'd have eaten hours ago if I'd known. But there was an upside. I served myself dinner on a tray and sat in front of the television, my happy little hand clutching the remote control. *I have you all to myself.* And I switched to CNN.

During the week, Santiago began attending Happy Hours with former classmates and meetings of the runners' and cyclists' clubs. Chileans dubbed these groups of men friends who meet regularly as the "*Club de Toby*," after Tubby in the comic strip "Little Lulu," who had his club of neighborhood buddies. I've learned to live with the Club de Toby. That's just how it is. I have my occasional nights out, too, and I've come to cherish those after-work hours and weekend mornings as precious time for myself to write, take a walk and garden. Solitary activities, true, but I enjoy my own company. Yet — I wouldn't mind a walking partner who lived close by.

The Spanish word *vieja*, meaning old woman or over forty to the younger Chilean generations, is often used here as an insult, sometimes followed by an unmentionable adjective, a favorite of men behind the steering wheel. Now well into the vieja category, I must work to maintain my self-esteem in this youth-oriented society. Clothes shopping is a downer, everything designed for teeny boppers, with the emphasis on the teeny. This is not a culture that venerates its elders.

For years, lacking models in the local media, I resorted to American magazines to find stories of women I could emulate and admire, whose lives would encourage me to aim high and pursue my dreams, women about whom I could think: *I hope to be like her someday, a Maxine Hong Kingman or a Joan Baez.*

Not my mother. A model too close to home. Marge, a former teacher colleague of my mother's, once summed her up this way: On Mondays, returning to work, they'd ask each other how their weekend was. Marge told of the country excursions she and her husband had taken. My mother listed with satisfaction all the tasks she had accomplished at home, an archetype of the Biblical Martha. Knowing this, I strove to be a Mary, more focused on people. But Martha qualities kept surfacing. Only years later did I recognize and feel good about the many ways I'd come to resemble my mother and appreciate that she was an avid reader, intellectually curious, politically active and deeply concerned for the needy and the environment.

After my father died, my mother began to visit us at Christmas. "You'll have to come every year," I told her. "And I'll visit you every July." We'd begun a new cycle.

One December was marked by special occasions: Nico's graduation from eighth grade, my fiftieth birthday and Danny's high school graduation. Danny excelled as a student, which helped compensate for any of the school's shortcomings. He had one unpleasant experience in his junior year when a teacher accused him of letting a classmate copy from his test paper. Danny insisted he was innocent, but we were called in to the "inspector's" office. I went prepared for battle.

The inspector sat behind his desk. "Señora, you must sign this paper and Daniel will be on conditional status this semester."

I bristled. "I'm not signing any paper. I believe my son. He doesn't deserve to be on conditional status. He's always been an excellent — and honest — student."

The inspector, an elderly, bespectacled man, referred to the handbook of school rules in front of him. "It says here in Article 325 B, Section IV . . .." He proceeded to read the rules to us.

What temptation to tell him what he could do with his rules. "Why should I sign when my son has done nothing wrong?"

We went round and round, he insisting on the rules and I on Danny's innocence. But I sensed that Danny was suffering. I told the inspector, "For the record, I'm in total disagreement, but I'll sign just to put an end to this." I'd compromised, but said my piece.

The school was a good fit for the boys. Their classmates included neighborhood buddies and sons of Santiago's former schoolmates. Here was their pass into the network and the contacts they'd need later in life.

We did not encourage Danny to apply to universities in the States. Not only was it financially difficult, we weren't ready to see our kids leave home yet. I'd become a Latina mother hen. Danny was accepted into the Universidad Católica, where he chose to study civil engineering.

The previous school year, a speech-language pathologist friend called offering me an opportunity to tutor Stephen, an American boy with Down's syndrome. He was enrolled at the international school where I had taught previously, which had no specialist teachers to meet his needs. Stephen was a delight. My friend worked with his language development, while I taught him writing and spelling. In return, he challenged me as a teacher to develop an eclectic variety of activities that would enable him to develop his unmapped potential.

The school board, taking notice that I was acquiring more private students besides Stephen, offered me a job as a learning disabilities teacher. I was reluctant to take on a full-time job with Nico still in school, yet, I wanted to develop professionally and knew the opportunity might not come again. I accepted, my life taking on a new focus and a hectic, but stimulating pace. I was to establish the first program for the learning disabled at the school. They sent me to observe the program at the international school in Sao Paulo. Later, I attended specialized workshops in Paraguay, Aruba and Florida. I loved my job and the flexibility granted me in the creation of a new program.

The following year the school hired a reading specialist — creative, enthusiastic, generous Anne. We soon became steadfast friends. Extremely conscientious, the two of us spent hours examining how to develop the skills of the children who lagged behind, many of whom were non-native English speakers. Were they candidates for an ESL program or LD support? It was a fine line. I was particularly drawn to the diagnostic facet of the job and loved the challenge of putting together the pieces of the puzzle. However, by returning to full-time teaching at the international school, I was limiting my opportunities to connect with Chilean women outside of the American school community.

The exceptions were the wives of Santiago's closest friends. One evening, while the men entertained each other with their stories at one end of the living room, we slipped into girl talk: the merits of Prozac and exercise classes, worry over 30-something kids who were still unmarried and pointers from the book *Men Are From Mars, Women Are From Venus*. Laughter. One confided the gap between her interest in sex and her husband's, revealing her unique non-verbal techniques for communicating "No interest tonight." More laughter. Another related a recent trip to Egypt and Turkey with two girlfriends. Listening to them, I thought: You've come a long ways, baby. Move over Chilean Tobys. Make way for us Little Lulus.

SUZANNE ADAM

The Morning with Oscar

Frost is sparkling on the ground and rooftops as Oscar, our occasional gardener, pulls up in his 1992 beige Volkswagon van. I hear the van chugging to a stop and I sigh in relief. He's arrived. I say "occasional" because he's a no-show more often than not, not unusual in Chile where gardeners are as unpredictable as spring weather. I put up with his unreliable ways because he and I are botanical soul mates.

Clad in baggy khaki pants, blue flannel shirt and baseball cap, he slides open the van's side door. He's brought me a present, *un regalo*, he says, pulling out a rectangular plastic pot, planted with a variety of herbs: mint, cilantro, thyme, oregano, dwarf celery.

Surprised, I thank him, though I suspect it's his way of apologizing for his absences.

Today we need to prune the bougainvillea, I tell him, and the lemon tree needs shaping. We discuss which branches to prune to allow more sunlight to play through.

Problems had kept him away, he says, poking at the dichondra declaring it's looking good. Just wait 'til spring, he says. The garden will be beautiful. He clops about in his thick work boots leaving a trail of mud clods on the patio. Oscar put this garden in for me last spring and takes an interest in how everything is faring. Planning and planting it was our mutual labor of love.

High on the ladder, he wrestles with the thorny bougainvillea, snips away, and tosses the branches down to the ground, and we chat. I ask him about insect repelling plants and ones that will attract ladybugs. I bring him coffee (three teaspoons of sugar) and wire to tie up bundles of branches.

Oscar is not a big man but he's strong and fit. He breaks up the branches with his rough hands, dirt caked underneath his finger nails. I ask why he doesn't wear gloves. He works better with his bare hands, he says. I empathize, being a no-glove gardener myself, the sense of touch guiding me to work tender roots into the soil.

"Oscar, *por favor*, if something comes up and you can't make it, call me."

"Sí, señora," he says. "I'll be back in fifteen days."

He lurches off in the van, and I look about my garden with satisfaction. He has waved his magic wand and coaxed the beauty out from under winter's ravages. Soon spring will tiptoe in and round out Oscar's magic.

9

My Country Tis of Thee . . .

Dulce Patria

The winter morning air was crisp, a sharp wind blowing. It was July Fourth in Chile, but not a holiday. Santiago was at work, while I stood in line at the American Embassy entrance. The guard passed his detector wand around my body, a strange way to start my country's Independence Day. What would Thomas Jefferson have thought? I flashed my passport and moved through the turnstile.

In line, I chatted with Rachel, who was also alone.

"My kids had exams at school today," she said, "but I wanted to come anyway."

I nodded. "I used to bring my boys when they were little, though some years we've been in the States for the Fourth."

Rachel smiled. "My last Fourth of July there I went to a baseball game!"

I understood her enthusiasm. "Once I took my boys to a parade near my hometown. Small town spirit was still alive. Everyone came out: Boy Scouts, firefighters, businessmen, politicians, flag-waving onlookers — a glimpse of Americana for my boys."

"I can't believe I've been living in Chile now for twenty-two years," she said. "My kids, totally Chilean, tease me about my accent."

I laughed. "Often I can't understand my own kids when they speak Spanish, and I've lived here longer than in the States."

I never imagined I'd be saying that one day.

Bundled in parkas, we were a mixed group in the embassy courtyard: expatriates, Mormons, students, bi-national families. Five young Marines, impeccable in dress uniforms, strode in formation to the flagpole. I could almost see my reflection in their polished black shoes. They solemnly unfolded and raised the immense flag, bright and bold. Beyond the fluttering flag glowed the ridges of the snow-clad Andes. The Chilean Army Band struck up the "Star-Spangled Banner." Images of the America of my memories flashed before me: picnics, football games, Girl Scouts, Peanuts comic strips, Norman Rockwell, Joan Baez.

A minute of silence for the Armed Forces in Iraq and Afghanistan was followed by a reading of the President's address to the nation, and, finally, a sing-along. How long it had been since I'd sung "It's a Grand Old Flag" and "Yankee Doodle Dandy." Over coffee, hot chocolate and cookies, I chatted with friends and met a newly arrived California woman. I was one of the last to leave.

My July Fourth wasn't over. Ann had invited us to dinner. I told her that Santiago had another engagement. "Come anyway," she said. So I did. Eight of us, Americans and Chileans, gathered in Ann and John's living room. John played his dulcimer and Ann her flute, as Rosita sang "Come Thou Fount of Every Blessing," a hymn sung in the times of the Declaration of Independence.

Around a table set in red, white and blue, John gave thanks for our blessings. Dinner was served on blue and white china commemorating America's bicentennial. Under my lasagna I discovered Independence Hall. Betsy Ross was hard at work on her flag on my coffee cup. Boston's North Church tower lay beneath my apple crisp. John told the Chileans of Boston's warning lantern code:

> One, if by land,
> And two, if by sea;
> And I on the opposite shore will be . . ..

"*Paul Revere's Ride!*" I said. "Henry Wadsworth Longfellow," remembering the book of Longfellow's poetry on a living room shelf of my family home.

Carmen recited her favorite poem by Robert Frost, "Stopping by Woods on a Snowy Evening," completing all four stanzas. Cheers and applause. We turned thoughtful when John read African-American poet Langston Hughes' "I, Too, Sing America" that began "I am the darker brother . . .."

Nothing would replace memories of July Fourth in Marin County — the summer warmth, grilled hamburgers, the picnic table set in patriotic colors on the deck, fireworks over the Bay. But that day I added a new rich layer to my memories — one fitting for someone who considered two countries home.

Two months later, I was commemorating a September independence day.

A small square of red paper looped and dipped, frolicking in the air currents, as if looking for escape into the blue sky. The string was not visible, but I saw the child treading new green grass as he worked the string, arms pumping. It was kite season in Chile. Bright harlequin squares soared over city parks and country fields — anywhere with a bit of open space — announcing the coming of spring. The dance of the kites swept my spirits upward, weary of winter's grey cloak. The air pulsated with the rhythm of folk songs on the radio and in supermarkets. Independence Day Week, Fiestas Patrias, was approaching. Anticipation filled the air, mingling with the mouth-watering aromas of the season's first barbeques. The mood was contagious, stirring me to hum along to those songs depicting life in the countryside, el campo, where the Chilean soul had its roots. I went to the attic to pull out this country's flag.

The bag boy at the supermarket asked: "Where are you from, señora?" My accent sparked curiosity. "I'm *norteamericana*, from California," I answered, a radical switch from what I'd tell my friends as a child. "I'm half Scottish, a quarter Dutch and a quarter German." My paternal grandfather immigrated at age thirteen to Canada from Holland with his older brother, never returning home or seeing the rest of his family again. Nor did I hear him speak Dutch or talk about his family. Too wrapped up in my young life to appreciate his stories, I failed to ask about his roots.

My mother often recalled when, at age six, she and her younger sister went by ship to Scotland with their mother and Aunt Anne, both of whom had left Scotland at a young age. She told me how Great-aunty Belle scrimped and saved out of their food money for years, so that her husband, Uncle Will, a radio repairman, could visit Scotland to see his mother. My immigrant grandparents, aunts and uncles seemed to have wholeheartedly embraced their new land, so much so that I never thought of them as immigrants. I never sensed that they longed for the "old country." Now I wonder if they harbored the same regrets and doubts that I feel here, but that, in their stoicism, they never expressed.

Am I an immigrant? An expatriate? Maybe both. I feel "gringa," as if the word were stamped on my forehead, like a plastic fever indicator, flashing a big G. I am perceived as different and feel different, a fact that poses frequent challenges to my self-esteem.

Citizen of the United States and "permanent resident" of Chile, I've lived a double identity, my feet straddling two continents. I vote in U.S. federal elections by absentee ballot, and with the return of democracy in Chile, as a permanent resident, I am permitted to vote. My first vote in Chile was to approve the new Constitution in 1980, followed by the 1988 Plebiscite to determine if Pinochet would continue governing for another eight years.

Chile's recent history is part of my history now. I can no longer claim to be a simple observer. Though a firm believer in democracy, I voted "*Sí*" in Pinochet's plebiscite, a vote for him to continue as president, because, like many others, I feared that a "No" vote meant a return to the violent pre-coup years. The same old politicians that brought Chile to the verge of civil war were hovering in the wings. I didn't trust them. But the No votes won and in 1990 General Pinochet handed over power to the newly-elected president, Patricio Aylwin, a Christian Democrat, a candidate of the same coalition of parties that put Marxist Salvador Allende into power.

The military government lasted for seventeen years — all of my boys' childhoods. The country's increasing economic stability and well-being lulled many into a level of comfort and acceptance. The curfew was modified and later rescinded. In spite of sporadic anti-military insurgent attacks, we felt safe. We became accustomed to hearing the blasts of explosions in the night, directed at offices of public utilities, foreign interests or military installations. High-tension power line towers being popular targets, I kept candles on hand for the frequent blackouts.

When Nicolás was five-years-old, he heard us talking of a bomb exploding on the Metro. For months after, he was afraid to board the subway, holding my hand tightly, asking, "Mommy, how many more stations to go?"

"Just three," I said and together we counted until we reached our stop.

With the return of democracy, I listened to Chileans struggle with unanswered questions and strive towards reconciliation. Events of the past were being brought to the forefront and discussed openly. The missing persons now had names and faces. Human rights. Justice. Pardon. Guilt. Innocence. Responsibility. Weighty words that resounded repeatedly in the media and in conversations. Truth. Perhaps the most difficult one of all. Was there one single truth about the past?

September 11th, once a holiday commemorating the coup, later became the occasion for rock-throwing young protestors and vandals to take to the streets to protest an event and a regime they never experienced. A statue to Allende was erected in the Plaza de la Constitución. History was rewritten again and again, tinted by the lens of the writer's political persuasion and by the government in power.

I was a political science major in college, but here I experienced first-hand, eye-opening lessons in politics and government. I struggled with my conscience. As I read alarming accounts of those who suffered unjust imprisonment, torture, and exile, I felt saddened and shaken. How could I have been unaware of what was happening? The limited access to accurate information had biased my thinking. For the first time I understood the importance of the First Amendment I'd studied in civics class. The coup may have been necessary, but the military government lasted too long. Only years later, was I able to acknowledge that the United States government was involved in Chilean politics of the time.

Faced with more complete information, the era of my political innocence came to an end. Yet, from all I observed and lived during those times, I believe the events preceding and immediately following the coup were primarily the makings and responsibility of the Chilean people and their political parties.

Although it is no longer obligatory to vote in Chile, I voted in the most recent presidential election. My polling station was a neighborhood school. Pedestrians streamed along the sidewalks while honking cars were backed up the street. Reporters, television cameramen and uniformed *carabineros* crowded the entrance. I located table 46 in one of the classrooms and joined several women in line. No men here; they voted at separate polling stations, though that would soon change. In the booth I marked my ballot, folded it into four parts, closed it with the stamp provided and dropped it into the ballot box. I then signed the official book and pressed my thumb to the ink pad, preventing me from voting a second time. In the evening, I watched the election returns with family and friends, feeling the mounting suspense and excitement.

Just months earlier, my visit to California coincided with the presidential elections. I'd already voted by absentee ballot, but went with Barbara to her polling place and sensed the tension in the air. In the evening, riveted to the television, we followed the returns of that history-making election. Witnessing Obama's triumphant speech, euphoria swept through me, inspiring a renewed pride in my country.

Like family or hair color, nationality was not something I chose or thought much about. Yet, how I perceive myself and the world is rooted in my American past. Living in Chile, being American became a conscious, integral part of who I am.

At times, surprising memories surface: shreds of phrases from American jazz and swing classics on Santiago's CD collection: "On the Sunny Side of the Street" and "Sentimental Journey" and Broadway musical tunes of the '50s: "Carousel," "Oklahoma," "Showboat," often played on Chilean radio stations. Sometimes, when out for a walk along the city streets, I'll sing songs from Girl Scout camp days, songs portraying America's folk heroes — Negro spirituals, sea shanties, cowboy lullabies:

> My home's in Montana,
> I wear a bandana,
> my spurs are of silver,
> my pony is grey.
> While riding the ranges,
> My luck never changes,
> With foot in the stirrup
> I'll gallop away.

SUZANNE ADAM

I miss having someone to sing my songs with. So few people here with whom I can share that nostalgia. Friend Donald was one — until he moved back to the States. I teasingly called him "*el viejo gringo.*" Married to a Chilean, we belonged to the same generation and had in common a parochial education and the Peace Corps experience. He would make me laugh, warbling '50s era radio and television jingles and theme songs for me to guess the commercial or the program. "Happy trails to you, until we meet again . . . ." Or we'd sing them together: "to look sharp and be sharp . . . .." Sometimes his face took on a sly expression to accompany an English adage appropriate to the moment: "He's not the sharpest tool in the toolbox." And we'd laugh, while our Chilean friends looked on perplexed.

Years of Catholic schooling are tucked away amidst mothballs in my cultural trunk: respect for laws, rules, and regulations, along with the mores of the 1950s. Living in the U.S., if the sign said, "Stay off the grass," I didn't even *think* about taking a shortcut. I'd stand in orderly lines and wait my turn at the bank or the post office, smiling and indicating to others to "please, go ahead." In Chile, I had to learn to defend my turn in the post office and meat market line. Yet, on the road, I feel guilty turning left before the green left turn arrow flashes, although no oncoming cars are in sight, making me feel mighty ridiculous here where a common attitude is: if you can get away with it, do it.

As a child, I became a bookworm and devoured the popular children's literature of the '50s: The Bobbsey Twins, Nancy Drew and *The Wizard of Oz*. Once we bought a television set, I tuned in to "Leave It to Beaver," "The Lone Ranger" and "Father Knows Best." Stories of the taming of the West, of pioneers, trappers, traders and explorers, captured my young imagination. Later, I soaked up California authors John Steinbeck, William Saroyan and Jack London.

Books, songs, stories. Those were the conveyors of the values of my society, defining the ideal family and women's role expectations, while promoting perseverance in the face of adversity, responsible citizenship and a strong work ethic. These were the stowaways in the baggage I carried to Chile.

As my boys grew older, I began to wonder: what was the American legacy I was passing on to them? When they were young, I sang them to sleep with "Home on the Range" and "Our paddles clean and bright . . ." but they've long forgotten those songs. They never read my father's childhood 1922 copy of *Huckleberry Finn*, gritty with dust on an attic shelf. In high school they did read *Tom Sawyer* and *White Fang* — in Spanish. Their only knowledge of my favorite part of U.S. history, the western frontier, was based on Hollywood movies.

One November I decided to celebrate Thanksgiving at home with a special dinner served in the dining room. In the past, with my American friends we'd organized Thanksgiving picnics, but with their families growing, they became too numerous to accommodate in someone's yard. I told the boys of my plans when they arrived from school and called Santiago at his office, asking him to come home earlier. Their reception was lukewarm. It was simply another work day, another school day. Santiago, buried in work, felt pressured to arrive home sooner than usual. My enthusiasm waned as I realized that I couldn't recreate the memories and the atmosphere of sharp fall days with a buttery sun and orange foliage, while here it was picnic weather. I was unable to convey the pleasures and significance the day had for me: my family — grandparents, aunts, an uncle and my two cousins — gathered at the table set with a starched, white tablecloth and freshly-polished silver, savory aromas of roast turkey and pumpkin pie wafting from the kitchen and a crackling fire in the living room. They had to have lived it.

Yet, Danny and Nico would never forget the introduction my father gave them to baseball. They jumped at any chance to go to the States for a visit or an extended stay and nothing kept them from grooving with American rock bands and following NBA basketball.

SUZANNE ADAM

My American-time expectations also failed to rub off onto Santiago and our boys. It wasn't simply a matter of asking everyone to come home earlier; the entire city functioned on a different schedule. Once I began working a full day, in the early evening I'd nibble my way through the refrigerator, harking to the grumblings of my gringa stomach. Then after our usual 9 p.m. dinner, I'd rush to get to bed, hoping to manage seven hours of sleep in order to face my students the next day. Then, after I'd set my alarm for 5:45 a.m. and settled into bed with a book, the phone would ring. For Nico. Then again. For Danny. The boys enjoyed an impressive social life, totally foreign to Santiago's and my experiences.

Next our boys were refining plans for the evening, running up and down the stairs to their rooms, grabbing music tapes and jackets and making more phone calls. Their interior clocks were set permanently several hours behind official parent time. At eleven p.m. Nico gave a brief summary of his plans and was out the door. Be home before midnight, we told him. A sigh and a despairing look. At 11:10 p.m. Danny took off. Having no early classes at the university, he was to be home no later than 3 a.m. The youth seemed to be gaining control in this society.

On Friday and Saturday, I knew I'd have my ears perked for their arrivals anywhere between three and five in the morning. Every passing car woke me. Was it stopping here? Was that the front door? Yes, one arrived. One to go. My stomach twisted into knots of anxiety, now that I was wide awake, afflicted with the insomnia I'd suffered during my post partum depression. Santiago wasn't happy with those hours, but he slept soundly through the night. The burden was on me to keep them safe — by worrying. The next day they'd sleep until noon, rankling at my rise-and-shine, make-hay-while-the-sun-shines American work ethic.

At the dinner table one night I asked Nico to repeat something he'd said. Sigh. Rolling eyes. Not again, I read in his face. Now that they were older, Danny and Nico were speaking Spanish with each other and with Santiago. I knew it wasn't that my hearing was failing. I suggested that they mumbled, but they didn't take me seriously. It was obviously me who had the problem. "Clean your ears, Mom." They had no clue that difficulty partaking in their conversations left me with a feeling of loss, of being an outsider in the family. And of looking stupid.

In his third year at the university, Danny applied to study an exchange semester abroad. His choice was no surprise: the University of California at Berkeley. Competition was stiff as there were just two openings. We were ecstatic when his acceptance letter arrived. He filled out forms for student housing. We waited, but no word came. It was July and classes started in September. Santiago and I had planned a trip to California that July. Now we had an urgent agenda — a trip to the student housing office.

We took the personal Chilean approach: explain the situation and ask for the person in charge. Would it work at one of America's largest universities? We were admitted to the director's office and explained to her that our son was arriving from Chile in six weeks and had nowhere to live. We spoke of our wonderful years as students there and how we'd met in Berkeley. She put his application on the top of the pile.

Danny shared a room with two others in one of the newer dormitory halls, similar to one where I had lived. My mother, also a Berkeley graduate, happily helped settle him there with all he needed. He grew a beard and let his hair grow long, just as his dad once had. When we talked on the telephone, I'd hear the familiar dorm sounds, reliving my university days vicariously, although there were changes. The dorms were co-ed now and a large part of the students were from other countries, like Danny.

When he returned after Christmas, I wanted to hear all about his time there. Minor details I preferred to overlook, like not washing his sheets the whole semester. The positive gains far outweighed any deficiencies in his personal hygiene. He'd taken a course in American poetry, hoping to improve his English writing skills. One day he handed me a copy of a small book of his own poetry. My soon-to-be engineer son writing poetry in English! Some of my influence had rubbed off after all. The highlight was his recitation of Allen Ginsburg's "Hadda be Playin' on the Jukebox."

As an import, I'm on guard not to fall into the habit of criticizing or making comparisons, but sometimes I've slipped, prefacing too many statements over the years with, "In the United States, we . . .." How easy it is to place the blame for my nostalgia or frustrations on Chile's idiosyncrasies, just as my father blamed this country for taking me away. But blame is a dead-end road, taking me nowhere that feels good.

Once, before I could emerge from a subway car, a man began boarding, heading straight towards me. I firmly planted my hand on a handle by the door, blocking his way until I was able to step out of the car. Passing him, I commented on his lack of manners and then spent the next hour in a debate with my conscience, trying to justify my aggressiveness and anger. On the road, attempting to change lanes still has me fuming when drivers ignore my signal. But, knowing I can't reform them, I try to remember my mantra: *Go gently.* When someone does slow down, I give them a thumbs-up.

Public manners, while on the endangered species list, are not extinct. I'm appreciative when a man in a crowded subway car offers me his seat (*do I look that old?*) and when men wait for me to emerge first from an elevator. If a driver stops for me at a crosswalk, I smile and wave and think the world is good.

One Sunday I spent the afternoon as an armchair tourist, watching a weekly series of television documentaries showcasing Chile's landscapes and culture: a bay on the northern coast inhabited by penguins, sea lions and whales; a prehistoric marine fossil found by a young Chilean paleontologist in Patagonia; artisans in country towns: a blacksmith, a family of basket weavers, a potter. This growing movement to promote appreciation for what is authentically "Chilean" pleases me. But it continues to be an uphill road when faced with the invasiveness of American culture, which, like a non-native weed, snuffs out what is local. At Christmastime, when temperatures are in the 80s and the sweat is dripping off of their faces, Chilean shoppers in the malls are entertained with the voice of Bing Crosby singing "White Christmas," and poor Santa is clad in a thick red suit. Hearing Bing Crosby takes me down memory lane, but what can it mean to the average Chilean who doesn't understand the words and has never experienced a white Christmas?

Though I applaud the promotion of Chilean culture, I often turn to Radio Oasis, 102.1 FM, where the voices of The Mamas and the Papas singing: "All the leaves are brown and the sky is grey . . . ." evoke my California days. And when they play "Mr. Sandman," my father's song, I turn up the volume and sing along.

Yet it's not long before reality interrupts my nostalgia.

Early one quiet summer morning a truck loaded with fruits and vegetables parked in front of our house. A grating, nasal voice shouted through a bullhorn: "I've got potatoes, carrots, squash, ripe peaches, lettuce, avocados." After this went on for several minutes, I went out to talk to the vendor. "Do you know that using a loudspeaker on city streets is illegal?"

"Señora," he replied, "we are in Chile."

Spring

The neighborhood is a floral explosion of purple, perfuming the air. I'd like to thank the wisteria blooms. Would they hear me?

Several ladybugs have taken up residence in the garden. I wish they'd invite their cousins to feast on our abundant supply of green crawly aphids.

Today I heard the delicate trill of the first white-crested eleania of spring. I've jotted down the arrival dates of these tiny birds for several years, always in September. I'm in awe of their timing and stamina, traveling from as far as the Amazon Basin.

Luminous puffs of clouds skim across a deep, azure sky, lifting my spirits. Too few skies like this bless our city days. The two Judas trees in front of our house are bursting in deep pink blooms. Their name derives from a legend that Judas hung himself from this tree. Not a pleasing connection.

Santiago is up on the ladder rustling amidst the branches of the avocado tree, wresting down big hard avocados with a long pole. My job is to hold the ladder and avoid being knocked unconscious by a falling avocado. It's hard to believe that Nico planted this tree from a seed. Now Santiago turns to the lemon tree and plucks a bagful of lemons. Our city garden harvest.

I'm off to the garden expo, Jardinera. It's a heartening sight to see hundreds of people and families with children enjoying the plant and garden displays, a striking contrast with yesterday's scenario at the former Congreso Nacional downtown: screaming students, faces contorted in anger, interrupting a congressional budget meeting.

10

Introduced Species

Especies Introducidas

With my forehead pressed against the plane window, I watched the passing landscape below, the red earth of the southwest, dotted by pinnacles of rock and bare plateaus. Which state was that below me now? New Mexico? Utah? Nevada? I was in awe of that vast expanse. *My country*. I wondered how many times I'd made this journey from the bottom of the world back to Marin County. Twenty? Twenty-five? Yet, each trip was like going home for the first time.

With my boys older, I began flying to the States every year on my own for educational workshops and visits with my mother. Those solo trips allowed me time to reflect on the double life I was leading, so betwixt and between, still deeply divided.

Crossing the Sierras triggered memories of family camping vacations, and I watched for familiar landmarks. The flight path took us over Yosemite Valley, and as we drew near, I stood up in the aisle, leaning over passengers for a glimpse of Half Dome. Then we were over the San Joaquin Valley and its sprawling towns whose names I no longer remembered. But, then, ahead, the familiar hills of San Francisco took shape in the distance. Excitement and expectation filled me. The plane descended toward the Bay waters and bounced onto the runway. *Hello, California.*

Stepping out of the airport, the smells of vegetation reached into the deep recesses of my earliest memories, evoking a stabbing nostalgia. Going north across the Golden Gate Bridge and into the Marin County countryside, those childhood fragrances grew more intense — dry summer grasses and oak, bay, madrone and redwood trees.

My mother was waiting for me in our family home, built by my parents in 1947. It was a gift to have this house to come home to. Both of us had looked forward to this visit for months. We hugged and looked each other over. Were there any changes? I wheeled my suitcases with their SFO baggage tags into my old bedroom and looked around the house, which had its own spicy scent of dried eucalyptus leaves. My mother had placed a vase with flowers from the garden on the dining room table, and I knew there'd be a cookie tin filled with brownies in the kitchen cabinet. I stepped out onto the wooden deck with its view of Ross Valley and, beyond, softly sloped Mt. Tamalpais. The deck sparked images of family meals, conversations with friends and cooling summer drinks. It was a warm day. "Let's have lunch out here," I said. Renewing the tradition of past visits, we carried placemats, sandwiches and cold drinks out to the deck table. Penny, the neighbor's dog, barked at a passing car. We talked as crickets chirped and cicadas droned, singing of the lazy days of summer. I told my mother about the learning disabilities workshop I'd attended and how the boys were spending their winter vacation. A blue jay squawked from a branch overhead, while from the underbrush, I heard the repetitive two notes of a towhee. My love of birds started here. There was always a birdfeeder in the backyard and books on a living room shelf for identifying our feathered visitors. Their songs and calls formed part of the essence of this place to me.

As I walked about the garden, my gaze took in the terrace walls my father built with smooth cobblestones that once paved the San Francisco Embarcadero. How the pine tree in back had grown! And there was the tall white oak, sunlight playing through its scalloped leaves, its crusty branches reaching protectively over the roof of the house.

Ethereal presences — younger versions of our family and me — populated the rooms, phantom moths fluttering in the closet of my memory. Faces looked silently from framed photographs on walls and tabletops. That house and its surroundings encased my growing years like a seedpod, releasing me when I was ready, but always there when I returned. That place — the house, the valley, the hills I once roamed, the mountain — had left an indelible imprint that was with me wherever I went.

Yet — at first, I felt like a modern Rip Van Winkle. Out of step. While at the conference in Florida, I attempted to make a long distance call to California.

"This is Cindy," said the operator. "With which company do you wish to make the call, ma'am?" naming a series of companies I'd never heard of.

Since when did we have to choose a company? "Uh . . . I haven't the slightest idea, Cindy. Whichever one is fine. You choose."

I didn't own or know what to do with a phone card. When people referred to an ATM, an ENT or an HMO, I stopped to think what the letters stood for. Nor did I know the names of the mayor or the hottest author or the host on the Late Show. On the phone, my friend Vreni gave me detailed explanations and highway numbers, which I wrote down, to get to her house in the East Bay, an area I once knew well.

As the days passed, my confusion and detachment faded. I went outside to renew my ritual of watering the garden, playing at living here once more, no matter how briefly. Our neighbor, George, came by walking his dog, Bobbie Burns. George stopped to chat, and I was pleased he remembered me.

SUZANNE ADAM

I petted Bobbie Burns. I went to exercise classes and contacted old friends. Eileen, a former teaching colleague, and I were to meet in Berkeley, where we both had studied. What a high I felt crossing the Richmond-San Rafael Bridge over the Bay, a silver sheet shimmering in the sunlight. A subversive thought, or maybe a realization, overtook me: *Look what I've been missing. Stop!* chimed in my conscientious, practical self. *No comparing countries. Just savor the moment.*

Eileen had just returned from teaching for three years in Manila. We actually found a parking lot with a space, but burst into laughter at our helplessness. There we were, two teachers, reasonably literate, attempting to follow the instructions for feeding dollar bills into the parking lot machine, but the machine stubbornly spit our money back.

"How about we leave a note on the windshield?" suggested Eileen.

"I don't know if that will work here," I said, both of us insecure in this changed society. We tried again until the machine finally swallowed the bills.

In the following days, like a whirling dervish, I visited San Francisco's De Young Museum, lunched with old classmates, took the ferry across the Bay and long walks through town, shopped and drove to the beach to fly kites with my oldest friend Paula. Americans' friendly manner impressed me. When I walked around our old neighborhood, strangers greeted me. The cashiers at the United Market asked me how I'd been, saying "Have a good day" like they meant it. I went for breakfast to Hilda's Coffee Shop and sat on a round red plastic stool at the counter, ordering hash browns, waffles, sausages and French roast coffee — my idea of heaven. Busy waitresses chatted with their regulars, the place buzzing with conversation. The man next to me noticed me peeking at the headlines of his newspaper, and soon we were commenting on the story. Then I knew why my father had been a Hilda's regular.

The next weekend four friends from our student days in

Berkeley got together at Barbara's house in Hollister. She and I were in the Peace Corps together. I hadn't seen the others in over thirty years, yet we fell into easy conversation about the days when we looked great in long, straight hair and bell-bottom trousers, and shared joys and dramas of current love affairs over mugs of coffee.

"Remember the night we drove over to Anne's apartment in San Francisco and smoked pot?" The few times we had tried grass had been in each other's trusted company.

"It was the three of us in Barb's green Beetle." We each picked up different threads of the story.

"And, afterwards, we went out to a Chinese restaurant."

"We did?" I scanned my fuzzy memory. "I don't remember that. What sticks in my mind is starting back over the Bay Bridge that night and seeing one of those enormous billboards displaying a big chunk of beef. Its bloody redness jumped out at me."

Gathered round the candlelit table, we raised our goblets of Chilean merlot.

"To us! To friendship!" We clinked glasses.

"*Salud* to Suzanne who has come all this way to see us!"

My eyes took in each one of their faces. "To all of you who are my lifeline to this place." I didn't want this weekend to end.

Someone uncorked another bottle. "Let's do this every year when Suzanne comes. We're never too old to have pajama parties."

Amid the laughter, the recollections and the catching up on our lives, I was delighted that I continued to have much in common with them. Like a spider, driven by a deep, inner need, I was reinforcing the strands of my web that connected me to old friendships and places from my past.

Another day, Paula and I followed our yearly ritual, walking the trail to Phoenix Lake on the side of Mt. Tamalpais through stands of redwoods and lacy shadows cast by the bay and madrone trees. I treaded the soft earth and inhaled the mixed fragrances of the trees and the bleached, dry grass of the open hillsides. Memories of this place went deep: of fishing excursions with my father on summer afternoons, of wading in the creek chasing after water skaters with paper cups, of evening picnics with Paula's family and mutual friends, filled with laughter and singing:

> Irene, good niiiight, Irene, good night,
> Good night, Irene, good night, Irene,
> I'll see you in my dreams.

At the top of the earthen dam, where the lake came into view — a place where turtles sunned themselves on floating logs — I was drawn by a familiar, pungent scent that seemed to be the very essence of that place, those hills, the lake. On the slope of the dam, I identified some shaggy, green-turning-brown weeds as the source of the spicy smell and broke off a twig, slipping it into my pocket.

Scanning a book of Marin's native plants, I found it: a perennial covered with sticky hairs that emit a strong odor with small yellow flowers at the apices, found in waste places, disturbed sites, and sunny hillsides. It's name was Chile tarweed, *madia sativa*, a member of the sunflower family. Native to Chile and California. Just like me.

But, how could that weed whose fragrance I identified so closely with my California hills also be a native of Chile? Perhaps some seeds snuck aboard a Spanish ship sailing up the Pacific coast in the 1700s, or, during the Gold Rush, when California-bound ships stopped in Chile to take on passengers. Or maybe a few seeds were carried in the pocket of a woman who wasn't sure where she belonged.

The countdown began. A week left. Five days. Four. Three. I checked my "to do" list. Run down to Trader Joe's for chocolate chips. Somehow I'd squeeze them into my bulging suitcase along with some family mementos: a silver platter, Aunty Belle's long, white, 100-year-old christening dress and a black and white photograph of my father and me fishing when I was four years old. Things my mother no longer wanted.

"I try to get rid of one thing each day," she told me. She said she was clearing out the house of its years of accumulations. She had a long way to go.

Two days. Make the last phone calls. I began to dread the goodbyes. The day before departure I told my mother that I was going for a walk. Her flat, "Oh," filled me with guilt for the moments I spent away from her. I followed Knoll Road to the top of the hill. The northern side of the hill looked down on the cemetery where we buried my father's ashes. From that vantage point, I gazed west over the rounded, sun-bleached hills, south to San Anselmo in the valley below, Mt. Tamalpais, its backdrop, and east towards San Francisco Bay. I held onto the moment, drinking in the panorama around me, with the intent of carrying those images back to sustain me until the next visit.

Once, when I had just recently arrived in Chile, I met an American woman who had been here twenty years. I asked her, "How often do you get back to the States, Dottie?"

"Oh, the last time I think was ten years ago," she said.

"Ten years!" I was incredulous. "Why so seldom?"

"It's easier that way."

Now I understood. As the plane climbed into the sky over the Bay, I craned my neck to get my last glimpses of the mountain, the City, the Golden Gate. The memory of my mother's tearful, crumpled face as she waved goodbye weighed heavily. The friends I'd parted with were going about their business as usual in the shrinking landscape below me, but I was no longer a part of that scene.

Back in the city, with the passing of the days and the months, family, friends and job anchored me here, keeping me from floating off into the realm of nostalgia and regrets. Nico started at the Universidad Católica where Danny was finishing his last year in engineering and planning a year of world travel after graduation.

Travel was clearly in the male gene pool of our family. As were sports. The two activities complimented each other, and I learned to take advantage of that.

One January, Santiago and I cruised south along the Pan-American Highway with two road bikes strapped on the back of our car. I fantasized that one of the bikes was mine, imagining that the occupants of passing cars might think that I was a serious, experienced biker. The truth was that one of the bikes was Santiago's, the other belonged to Nico who'd meet up with us in Pucón on the shores of Lake Villarrica, the site of a yearly international triathlon. Santiago was to do the cycling portion of a relay with a mother-daughter duo, while Nico planned to compete in the three events, a Half-Ironman.

Adrenalin streamed through the streets of Pucón, the excitement and tension in the air contagious. Sidewalks swarmed with athletes and the streets with cars and pickups loaded with bicycles. Mud-splattered trucks and vans, announcing *"Desafío de los Volcanes,"* cruised by, topped with layers of kayaks. In addition to the tri-athletes, the participants in the "Challenge of the Volcanoes" competition were descending upon the town, after six grueling days of trekking, cycling, rappelling Andean peaks, and kayaking rivers in Argentina and Chile.

My role was family logistics manager, official photographer, cheerleader and equipment guardian. I became an old hand at this, helping squeeze bicycles, helmets, cycling and running shoes into our cramped hostel quarters, and draping sweaty shorts and tops over chair backs and lampshades. At the spaghetti feed in the evening, I put on a face of enthusiasm and listened patiently as Santiago, Nico and their buddies discussed former races, best times, recent injuries and current states of physical fitness. And I knew what to expect afterwards, a rehashing of the race, detail by detail — weather conditions, times, cramps, congratulations and laments — over lunch, over coffee, over dinner and on into the next day.

But I willingly put up with these inconveniences and mono-thematic conversations, for I'd discovered that my family's cycling and running competitions were my road trips. While they trained for the upcoming competition, I was free to hike, explore and meet other travelers with stories to tell.

As I walked along the main street in Pucón, one of Santiago's running pals called out to me:

"Gringa! Come! There is someone I want you to meet!"

I followed him to a sidewalk café where he introduced me to a young, red-headed American woman, named Sarah. I joined her at her table.

"What brings you here?" I asked. *What else would one gringa ask another when meeting in this country at the bottom of the world?*

"Kayaking," she replied.

Since I knew nothing about kayaking, nor had I ever met anyone who practiced the sport, I peppered her with questions. She had flown to Chile from Colorado with a group of friends and twelve kayaks. She briefed me on the ins and outs of the sport. I listened, captivated, as she described her group's perilous descent of the famous Futaleufú River in northern Patagonia. Not to appear totally ignorant, I told her about Pam Houston's book, *A Little More About Me*, which had a great kayaking story. As we said our farewells, I felt pangs of regret at not having lived such adventures, but experienced an exhilarating high at having rubbed elbows with a woman who had.

In the afternoon, as I soaked up sun in the hostel garden, two gorgeous hunks from Brazil, competitors in the "Challenge of the Volcanoes," emerged from the adjacent cabin and joined me. I pumped them for details about their experience, while secretly admiring their brawny physiques. Leaving them to their well-deserved rest, I donned my hiking boots, relishing the thought of having the whole afternoon to pursue my chosen activity. I trudged down a country road towards the Ojos de Caburgua waterfalls. Along the roadside, simple shrines — little statues and jars of flowers atop tables — sparked my curiosity. A passing campesino explained that the next day there would be a procession along there honoring their local patron, San Sebastián. Returning from the falls, I stopped by a roadside stand to admire baskets of raspberries being sold by a native Mapuche woman. She invited me into her *ruca* where her family was having tea. When I took leave, she handed me three gnarled green apples from their orchard.

My men had returned from their light training for the next day's Triathlon. They were in good spirits and ready for the big event. They laid out their clothes and set the alarm clock. I sensed their nervous anticipation and wished them a good night's sleep.

The day dawned clear and warm. I snapped photos as Santiago and Nico found their places and arranged their equipment at the starting point. Then — they were off! I zigzagged back and forth, squeezing between onlookers, positioning myself for a view of one or the other as they passed, but I had difficulty spotting them. In wet suits and caps, and cycling jerseys, helmets and lycra shorts, all the competitors looked alike. After completing the strenuous cycling segment of his relay, Santiago joined me to watch for Nico in the final running event — a half- marathon.

"Here he comes!" I pointed. "He looks tired . . . and in pain."

"*Vamos*, Nico! *Vamos!*" we shouted as he passed. He still had three laps to go. I ached for him.

Then, standing among the cheering crowd, I shot photos as he crossed the finish line. We rushed to congratulate him on completing his first Half-Ironman — one mile of swimming, fifty-six miles of cycling and thirteen miles of running. I oozed with maternal pride and soaked in the euphoria in the finishers' tent.

Some days later, as we headed north back up Route 5, I informed Santiago that I already had a destination in mind for our next trip. It would take us into more distant and unfamiliar territory — the Argentinean and Chilean Patagonia, where a bicycle was less practical baggage to take along. Required equipment would be two pairs of binoculars for our mutual addiction to bird watching. And I wouldn't mind if a pair of running shoes were tucked into his bag — that is, as long as next to them were a pair of sturdy hiking boots.

Upon Danny's return from his world travels, he took a job at an environmental consulting firm, pursuing his interest in ecology, which pleased me immensely. He moved into an apartment with two friends, breaking the Chilean tradition of living at home until married. But, it wasn't long before he met the right girl and married Alejandra.

My mother, then eighty-seven, made the long trip for the wedding. She had grown more unstable on her feet since I'd last seen her, while a wound on her leg from a recent fall was not healing well. I worried about her living alone in her hillside home, having no one to look in on her. She was becoming my responsibility. The idea frightened me.

Rain

Rain is forecast. The skies have loomed threatening since yesterday, but all we've gotten is an occasional teasing drizzle. It hasn't rained in seven or eight months, and experts predict another year of drought. I look at the clouds and make a silent prayer. *Please. Rain.* If we could understand the language of the trees and the ground beneath us, I imagine they're begging for moisture. I'm certain my redwood tree is.

How to describe the scent of rain? My nose recognizes that evocative fragrance triggering an accumulation of memories at the sensual level; my brain labels it rain, but that is not adequate. Poets compare the scent to things (earth, leaves) and emotions.

Then I find the word.

Petrichor — the smell of rain on dry earth. The term derives from the Greek words *petra*, meaning "stone" and *ichor*, which is the fluid that flows in the veins of Greek gods. The word was coined in 1964 by Australian researchers who found that the smell was created by an oil that is released by certain plants during dry periods. When it rains, that oil is released into the air, giving us that wonderful unique smell.

Perhaps it is really a collage of fragrances, unleashed when stone, leaf, earth, wood, cement are touched by rain. It takes on its greatest potency in the presence of vegetation, and each blade of grass, leaf and tree must have its own particular scent, creating a rich blend our noses recognize as rain.

At last. All the signs. A dark, threatening sky and icy wind. We'll have snow in the foothills, and the city will be encircled with a crown of white ridges. A profusion of dry sycamore leaves blow down our street, looking like an invasion of migrating crabs.

There it is. The soothing rhythm of falling drops, the plink-plink in the water spouts. "Itsy-bitsy spider" time. I smile in gratitude and relief.

11

Uprootings

Desarraigos

Once again, I heard the call of the flicker, that cousin to the woodpecker that takes up residence in Marin in the fall and winter. I trod hills thick with baby green grass and gave a silent shout of joy upon discovering the wild iris and pink and purple wildflowers I remembered from childhood. At last, after years, I beheld the California landscape in its spring and fall hues, under a different slant of the sun. But those trips to California were no longer the carefree summer sojourns of the past.

During a December visit to my mother when she turned 88, her physical deterioration was suddenly evident. It had been just seven months since her trip to Chile, but now she was having difficulty making it up the last of the house's fifteen steps. As I climbed the stairs behind her, I noticed her pulling herself up by the handrail. The dreaded time — that had always seemed a distant, nebulous point in the future — had arrived. She could no longer safely stay on alone in her house. Though she tenaciously drove around the county, watered the hillside garden, and maneuvered the stairs to get the mail and put out bottles and cans for recycling as she had always done, her strength was rapidly failing.

On previous visits, I'd gently broached the subject of her future. She'd even looked around for places to move, but neither of us expected the change to be so imminent. Always active and independent, she resisted accepting that she was no longer able to continue with her familiar routine. I had less than a month to convince her and make the move.

We went to see a two bedroom apartment available at the senior residence she had visited and liked.

"But I only need one bedroom."

"This is what's available now, Mother. Besides you'll be able to keep more of your things. Look. Here in the bedroom you'll have room for your dresser and both bedside chests of drawers."

"I'll have to buy a new bed," she argued.

"Yes, you will. And you can keep your small sofa bed for me when I come to visit."

"I'll miss my view of Mt. Tamalpais."

"So will I. But look. There's a garden right outside the bedroom window. At least it's not overlooking the parking lot." Her face was impassive. Days later, the pastor of her church and I finally convinced her that the move was for the best.

My mother wanted to sell the house. I couldn't bear to let it go. "Why can't we rent it?" I said. But arranging the move and getting her into a safe environment consumed all my energies. Dealing with rental issues was more than I could handle. In my many moments of doubt and indecision I thought: if I didn't live so far away, there might be another way out. Selling was the only realistic solution.

We contacted a real estate agent and a "For Sale" sign appeared outside like an unwelcome intruder at the house where I'd spent all my childhood, the home that I returned to on each trip back to California. When my parents built the house, the road was just a narrow gravel lane and Mr. Starkey's fig orchard was the view from the living room window. I was bereft and mourned as if I'd lost a beloved family member. That decision severed the umbilical cord that connected me to my childhood, to the memories, to that place — the hillside house on that parcel of earth in Marin County that was ours. It wasn't that my growing years there were complete bliss. I wouldn't forget the dark moments, but I'd forgiven long ago. The good feelings and memories overpowered the distressing ones. Now I felt my roots ripped from the land. I began saying to people, "I'm from . . . or "I grew up in . . ." seldom referring to California as "home." It was "home" only in my memories and my dreams.

In two weeks we sorted and sifted through fifty-seven years of accumulated family possessions. I'd hold something up to my mother and ask, "To keep or not to keep?" Books, clothes, dishware, boxes of photos and collections of vinyl phonograph records. It took me three days just to go through the Christmas decorations: tree ornaments, gift wrap and ribbons, unused Christmas cards, knit stockings, angels and Santas. I arranged to ship to Chile my mother's china, crystal, silver and other treasures she no longer needed but that I couldn't bear to part with. Two of my father's wooden duck decoys would guard our fireplace.

In our cold, dreary, catch-all basement I sifted through the contents of shelves and boxes with lingering reminders of my father: jars of nails, coils of wire, flower pots, bee traps and the tiny blackboard with the dates he'd last fertilized the tomatoes, written in his hand. In a bulging drawer of the wobbly orange and brown dresser I discovered black and white photos of different stages of the house's construction: an empty lot with the lone oak tree, my father and his friends pick-axing the stubborn hillside rocks to make way for a garden, the house's first Christmas, lightly powdered with snow.

The days prior to the move I trod an emotional tightrope, rushing against a time limit, exhausted, a wreck. Each morning I checked the multiple lists of things to do. So absorbed by our tasks, my mother and I had little time to think about the significance of what we were doing. Disoriented and overwhelmed by all the decision-making, she was emotionally flat, as if she had already closed that chapter in her life.

Yet, some special moments stood out those last few days. One night Paula brought over dinner, complete with tablecloth and candles. We lit a fire in the fireplace for the last time, and the three of us ate at a folding card table, surrounded by bare walls and piles of boxes. We recalled the good times and old friends that our families had shared over the years. Paula managed to keep us laughing in spite of our somber surroundings.

Another day, though mid-January, it was warm enough for my mother and me to have lunch on the deck. I gazed out at our view of the mountain, captured innumerable times in our photos, framed by the familiar oak and buckeye trees, and knew this would be our last time sitting there.

There was a funny moment — at least, looking back on it. I felt certain the scene tickled my father's sense of humor. The morning before moving day I woke to find my mother standing in the bathroom in her nightie, plunger in hand, attempting to coax the toilet to unplug, water swirling dangerously close to the rim. Her thin arms weren't up to the task.

"Mother! What on earth are you doing?"

"This damned toilet's plugged up."

"I can see that. Here. Let me give it a try." After some thought, I added, "But I can't do it with a full bladder."

With just the one bathroom in the house, I considered my options, then, throwing a jacket over my pajamas, I stepped out into the wintry air and headed for the bushes. As far as I could recollect, that was the only time I'd peed in my own garden.

Moving day.

A friend was to take my mother to her new apartment, while I'd stay back with the movers. But, before leaving, my mother did one last thing. Walking out onto the deck to the wooden planter filled with chrysanthemums, she pinched off the tips, as she had done every winter, to assure that they'd grow robustly.

Then she headed down those fifteen steps for the last time and out the front door, without looking back.

Once settled in her apartment, she only occasionally referred to the house.

"I don't know where those bank papers are. I used to keep them in the cabinet in the little bedroom."

"I miss my view of Tamalpais."

"My hibiscus doesn't get as many flowers. I have no sun here."

I went back to look at the house my next trip to visit my mother and was disappointed to learn that the new owners bought it as an investment, remodeled it and put it up for sale. I wasn't sure if I wanted to see it or not, but I couldn't stay away. A real estate agent was showing the house to a family with two children and was reluctant to let me in. I explained that I'd come from Chile and that my parents had built the house, it having been my family home for almost 60 years. She consented, explaining the situation to her clients.

The changes inside were drastic. I had to search for something familiar. The kitchen was now where the dining room had been, the redwood siding around the fireplace torn out, my parents' bedroom converted into a family room.

"How does it look to you?" the real estate agent asked.

They waited for my response.

"It's . . . it's very different now." I could barely get the words out. They rushed to bring me tissues. It was no longer the house I remembered — yet, it was.

Another day, during the week, I went back when no one was there and wandered around the garden and up the hill in back. The cobblestone wall my father built in the back garden was still there, but his brick barbeque and the wooden planter with my mother's chrysanthemums were gone. I said farewell to the trees, to the hill and to the house and picked a lemon for my mother from the tree she planted years ago. Though larger, the house from the outside still had the same "look," like a familiar face. Strange, but I continued thinking of it as ours, as though something of us would always remain there.

Not long after the move, my mother's health began to fail. She who was always so active had a great fear of falling and began using a walker. A gentle slope was a mountain in her eyes. She resisted the doctor's recommendation that she no longer drive. She continued to read, keep up on current events, and follow the local football teams on television, though she often nodded off to sleep in her favorite chair. She had difficulty remembering names or what she had just told me minutes earlier. I couldn't count on her for household tips or cooking advice. *How do you keep your Scottish shortbread from crumbling? How long should I cook the turkey?* She no longer retained in her memory information for which she had no use. *But your daughter needs it,* I wanted to shout.

My twice-yearly visits were never enough. So much to do. I took her to be fitted for hearing aids, yet sometimes ended up yelling after having to repeat myself several times. Then I had to deal with the guilt. There were multiple doctor appointments and medical exams, shopping for new shoes, pedicure, manicure. Lunch at the senior residence was at noon and dinner at five. I felt imprisoned, but it was only a month, I reminded myself, struggling to be patient with her slowness, her fears and her hearing loss. How difficult to accept that she was no longer the all-knowing, non-stop superwoman who had ruled our roost. Now I was the one organizing and giving orders: "Pull the walker closer to you, then you can stand up straighter," or "Take the walker into the bathroom with you." When I was being particularly bossy, she would put me in my place, retorting, "Yes, Mother!"

I insisted she buy a Power Lift Recliner Chair, after watching her struggle to lift herself out of her easy chair, thin arms and legs trembling with the effort. Later I secretly renamed the chair "The Hulk." My mother loved her old chair and didn't want to give it up. I said, "Let's just go take a look."

A sample recliner stood right inside the front door of Jack's Drug Store. The salesman had my mother sit and showed her how it worked. "It's so big," she objected. I knew her objections ran deeper than its size. The chair meant owning up to her increasing disabilities. But I was determined. Hers was a grudging, unspoken acceptance.

The hitch was teaching her to operate yet another remote control. "Look," I said. "Just press this button to get up and that one to sit back." After several practice sessions, she began to get the hang of it. She sighed in exasperation at my reminders, but I had to make certain she could function on her own once I was gone.

She developed a routine. On a small table beside the chair she kept the TV remote control, the wireless phone, a glass of water and a letter opener. Going through her mail took most of her afternoons, with time out for cat naps and "Jeopardy." The big, brown recliner made her life easier. It wasn't until later that I realized how much I disliked the chair. It reminded me of her decline.

When I was in Chile, we talked daily by telephone, or I talked with Patricia whom we hired to go twice a week to take my mother out, keep up with her bills and tax declarations, shop for her medications — and everything I would be doing if I were there.

My mother suffered a fainting episode during one of my visits, resulting in the first of many visits to the hospital emergency room. On a subsequent trip, I realized she needed daily care and contacted a local agency that guaranteed close supervision of its caregivers. I explained that I lived in Chile and depended upon someone reliable to meet my mother's needs.

From Chile, I talked to Soledad, the weekday caregiver by phone. She was from Mexico and we spoke in Spanish. But her schedule of four hours a day, five days a week meant that my mother was alone the rest of the time. There were more visits to the emergency room. The residence director called to tell me that my mother had fallen out of her chair. They encouraged me to move her to an *intensive care section*, dreaded words to my mother. But soon it was clear that she needed 24-hour care. The agency sent more caregivers, one for daytime, another at night and others on the weekends. They kept changing. Alma from Peru. Louise, Bertha, Nora from the Fiji Islands. I struggled to remember who was on duty and keep track of the hours and expenses.

For my mother this parade of women was even more bewildering. On the phone one night she said, "This big black woman showed up this evening. She wants to sleep on the floor instead of the sofa bed." There were days when I called my mother and asked to talk to the latest caregiver, Lola. "She didn't come," my mother answered. Panicked, I called the agency. They called the caregiver's cell phone and then returned my call. Lola was right there in the adjacent room or she was downstairs doing laundry.

She didn't seem to be making new friends at the residence and most of her old friends were gone. The members of her church were kind to her, helping to alleviate my guilt and worry.

To my relief, she had the occasional company of her peripatetic grandsons. Danny, then studying for his Masters' degree at Berkeley, visited her often with Alejandra and their infant twin daughters, Manuela and Colomba. Getting to know her great-granddaughters was the joy of her restricted life.

Nico, by then also a civil engineer, arranged to visit his grandmother when on vacation from his job as a guide in Torres de Paine National Park in Patagonia. From those far southern reaches at the bottom of the world he headed north.

Was it in their genes or was it my attachment to that place that rubbed off on my boys and drew them north? Would I lose them someday to the place I'd left behind?

Dealing with my mother's health issues long distance, plus the stress of my job, was taking its toll. Unexpectedly, the school administration announced that it was offering, on a trial basis that year, severance pay for those who had been hired in 1990 or later, and wished to retire. It sounded tempting. I was sleep-deprived and burned-out. My motivation for my job was at an all-time low. What had happened to me? I felt guilty. This was my chosen profession, my vocation, but I wanted out. I turned in my resignation.

There were many things I hadn't achieved yet in my life. I wanted to expand myself, branch out, explore without the confines of a school calendar and ringing bells. And my mother needed me. Now I could visit her more often and any time of the year.

This gift of time allowed me a welcome freedom. My days were filled with an array of options: coffee and conversation with a friend, tending the garden, traveling and writing. I'd tried my hand at poetry as a child, dreadful imitations of Robert Louis Stevenson's *A Child's Garden of Verses*. As a teacher, I'd worked to instill sparks of creativity in the writing of my young students, but teaching allowed little time to flex my own writing muscles, aside from sporadic journaling. One summer day, while reading Frances Mayes' *Under the Tuscan Sun*, a lightning bolt of realization struck me. I wanted to put on paper my thoughts about Chile: impressions, revelations, inspirations and doubts to which I needed to give voice.

I made a retirement plan: mornings dedicated to writing and afternoons to tutoring children. Simple enough. Sounded idyllic. Tutoring would help supplement my minuscule Chilean pension and provide my days with some structure as I adjusted to this amorphous element of time in my life. Four afternoons a week — Friday was for play — I headed to the homes of students from my former school with my bag of books, games, pencils and stickers. Without the pressure of never-ending reports, meetings and ringing bells, I applied my teaching knowledge and experience in the most satisfying scenario — one-on-one. And I was my own boss.

A magazine published the first article I'd ever submitted,

and my head swelled — until a series of rejections followed. The discipline and perseverance that writing required did not come easily to me, and household distractions gnawed away at my mornings. I discovered writing to be a solitary craft until I learned of an English-speaking writing group. The Thursday morning meetings of the Santiago Writers became the highlight of my week. When someone would ask me what I was doing, I'd reply, "I tutor." Then, in a quiet voice, I'd add, "I also write."

Writing Thursdays

We're a bunch of spirited women this morning. Eleven of us. Sue, our itinerant member, is here from Toronto, and Ellen is back from her travels in South Africa. Jennifer has made the trip from the coast.

The shiny new, hot-off-the-press copies of our anthology, *Perspectives*, are what have us all grinning and excitedly planning the next step.

At the book launch, we glow like celebrities. Our night of glory. The best part is my family meeting my writing friends and getting a glimpse into this facet of me.

Our Word of the Day: conundrum. Oh-oh. Not sure of its meaning . . .. A puzzle? I used to think I held a healthy stockpile of words in my memory, yet, daily, I encounter English words that leave me in doubt. I may have heard them or read them but don't use them. Is this a case of "If you don't use it, you lose it"? Living in a non-English-speaking country has rendered my English vocabulary geographically deprived. I turn to my trusty off-to-college gift: *Webster's New World Dictionary of the American Language, 1958 College Edition*, its red cover faded and spine loose and frayed. *Conundrum: a riddle whose answer is a pun; a puzzling question, a problem.* My current conundrum: is my aging memory capable of retaining new words when it has difficulty producing the old ones on demand?

Why do I write? Keep a journal and toil for years on my memoir? I live an ordinary life, yet I want to preserve the memory of the people and things I've loved: my granddaughters' questions on life, death and God; the beauty of the Marin hills; the cry of a blue jay, the scent of a redwood grove, the rush of wind on the Patagonian pampas. These shining moments fill me, and I feel compelled to pass on the joy to others. An inner drive propels me to create; words are my medium as clay is to the ceramist.

12

Like the Crustacean in its Shell

"Como el crustáceo en su caparazón . . ."

"Can we stop here?"

We were headed up the mountain in our Fiat ladybug on a fine summer day.

"*Qué pasa?* What's the matter?"

"This road . . .. Is there some spot where we can turn around?"

It was my first trip into the Andes.

I didn't want to offend Santiago. He wanted to impress me, driving us up the road to Farellones, the ski area that overlooked the city. He pointed out small glaciers in the distance, but the nearest white peaks were my knuckles. The dirt road wound like a snake up the mountainside — nearly vertical from my perspective — its forty hairpin turns numbered on yellow road signs. After curve twenty, we bumped along a straight ridge, bare cliffs on both sides plunging into deep canyons. I'd had enough and wanted desperately to return to something close to sea level.

He nosed the car to the edge and put it into reverse. I fixed my eyes out the rear window as we backed toward the abyss.

"When I was a teenager headed for a day of skiing," Santiago said, "I used to make this trip aboard a canvas-backed truck seated on a wooden bench."

Well, goody for you, I thought.

We ventured up again the following winter. The road was lined with walls of snow, the pavement icy and slick, the views magnificent. I was a disaster at skiing, but the worst was the journey. I clenched my fists and pressed my feet to the floorboard, counting the curves. Years later, the road would be paved, two lanes — if a faint yellow line painted down the center constituted two lanes – and wide enough so we needn't back up or down to let a car squeeze by – except on the switchbacks.

The oak-dotted, wheat-colored California hills as my inner frame of reference makes it difficult not to make comparisons with the familiar and the loved. I have to work at finding beauty in this city's surrounding dry foothills of scanty, brown grass, thistles and cactus.

Where are the trees? The lakes? The tingling fragrance of pine needles? I miss the sound of the wind murmuring through the firs and pines of California's Sierra Nevada. Memories of family camping trips along Glen Alpine Creek at Fallen Leaf Lake return to tease me. My mother and I slept outside, our sleeping bags resting on a bed of pine needles we'd gathered. I'd gaze at the starry night sky framed between the high tree branches. My father preferred the tent. Before dawn, he and I rose to go fishing at Lily Lake. He loved those mountains as much as I did.

With longing do I think of the redwood groves dotting Mt. Tamalpais and recall Robinson Jeffers' lines describing California's coastal mountains:

> Like the steep necks of a herd of horses
> Lined on a river margin, athirst in summer, the mountain ridges
> Pitch to the sea, the lean granite-boned heads
> Plunge nostril under . . .

Yet, if I lift my eyes higher here, above summer's sparse vegetation, to where the cordillera meets the sky, a dynamic scene is often unfolding — mushroom clouds, like flocks of sheep, are grazing the ridges. Sometimes I imagine the clouds as luminous, billowing sails of a fleet of ships navigating granite waves. From my backyard, I observe their slow graceful gathering and parting. In winter, weighted with moisture and ice, they turn dark and secretive, casting a grey pallor over the landscape. Sudden rolls of thunder from distant peaks suggest the presence of a hidden cannon from a long forgotten battle. I've learned to read the clouds and know when rain or snow is on its way.

Back when I was driving to work, the mountains were the first sight to greet me, the rising sun fanning out above the jagged outline in the eastern sky. During the school day, I was not content to simply watch the view from my desk. If I planned my time carefully, I could fit in laps around the track up the hillside. I wolfed down my lunch and put on my sneakers. "Anyone want to join me?" I'd ask my colleagues, but usually I was on my own. On those days, I listened for quail twittering in the underbrush. A small American kestrel sometimes eyed me from his perch.

At home, from our second floor, I have views of the cordillera in two directions. One clear day, the thick veil of smog having been swept away by a welcome breeze, the mountains loomed over the city, as if they had snuck in closer during the night. I picked out the rounded peak of *"El Plomo,"* "The Grey One," its glacier, at nearly 18,000 feet, capping its bald dome like a white beret.

Some afternoons, I climb the stairs expressly to witness the waning sun creating soft shadows of taupe, blue and pale purple in the depressions among the rocky folds. The barren mountains suggest something primitive, wild, rough, perhaps gigantic iguanas, the furrows of their creased skin, their legs and tails, forming the slopes and depressions, the crests of their heads and backs, ridges and peaks. In winter, the setting sun turns the snow-mantled peaks a glowing, pale pink.

SUZANNE ADAM

Living here, I have come to realize that I am a lover of places and that I never got over my first love, Marin County. Wallace Stegner wrote: "Whatever landscape a child is exposed to early on, that will be the sort of gauze through which he or she will see all the world afterward."

Climbing backyard trees, freely roving Marin's hillsides and walking to school along Ancha Vista canyon, which was inhabited by deer and squirrels, spoiled me. I couldn't wait for June to come, when I'd board the bus to Girl Scout camp for two weeks at Huckleberry Woods in Big Basin Redwoods State Park. There we slept on the soft ground under the redwoods, not like the pampered Camp Fire Girls down the road who slept in tents. In August, my father, mother and I would pack up Jerry, our Springer Spaniel, and all our camping gear — oh, the stuff we piled on the roof rack — to spend three weeks at Fallen Leaf Lake.

Recently, I came across tattered sepia photos of my grand-parents and my father hiking on Mt. Tamalpais. They had traveled from San Francisco by ferry — before the Golden Gate Bridge was built — and then by train to the German hiking club, *Die Naturfreunde*, Nature's Friends, on the slopes of the mountain. While I was growing up, my father took me fishing rather than hiking.

A few years ago, I climbed Mount Tamalpais for the first time. A soaring euphoria washed over me, sitting by the lookout at the top, barely able to absorb the breathtaking, wrap-around vision of hills, forests, bay and sea stretching out below. I inhaled the leafy, earthy fragrances deeply, savoring them. Like Max, our beagle — R.I.P., scents speak to me. Perhaps, as a city dweller, I suffer from sensory deprivation; then, when back in touch with the land, the *not having* allows me to be more aware of the little things — the play of sunlight through quivering leaves, the intense blue of the sky, the musky aroma of a creek cascading through redwood groves. That day I felt that, by treading those slopes and immersing myself in the scents of manzanita, oak and redwood, I'd created a special bond with that mountain that had been a constant presence in my childhood.

As I grew more accustomed to the steep, winding roads here, I looked for opportunities for trekking excursions, but there were many obstacles: household chores, kids to pick up, scanty information regarding local trails, but, mainly, a hiking partner. I lacked companions with the same interest.

Summers, after our boys were on their own, Santiago and I began to search for southern national parks with possibilities for trekking. Being an athlete, he discovered he enjoyed a challenging trail. Those were also occasions for bird watching.

One year, I found my first fossil high on a wind-swept plateau of the Patagonian Andes, standing in a field of marine fossils. With each step I scanned the ground for the best one, the most perfect. There: one with a clear imprint resembling a sand dollar in the center of a reddish circle. I thought of Charles Darwin. Almost two hundred years earlier, he too walked these ridges, collecting fossils and taking notes. He claimed he could hardly sleep at night for thinking of the magnificent workings of nature that produced these mountains. I tried to imagine the millennial process, the layers of sediment from the ocean floor lifting these marine fossils to the top of the plateau.

My first impression of the cordillera as foreboding wasn't totally off the mark. Recurring tragedies reminded me that the Andes possess their dark side and could be unforgiving. The December of our wedding SURVIVORS FOUND FROM URUGUAYAN PLANE CRASH filled the newspaper's front pages. Missing since the start of spring when the mountains were still covered in snow, hope of finding any survivors, members of an Uruguayan soccer team, had all but disappeared. But two young men departed the crash site and struggled for eleven days through the mountains until meeting up with a cattle herder, who alerted authorities. Faced with starvation, they and the other nine survivors had resorted to necrotic cannibalism.

Rescued by helicopters, by chance they were taken to the hotel where my parents were staying.

Some years later, Santiago and I flew south in a friend's Piper Navajo along the base of the mountains. Fertile valleys, crisscrossed by snow-fed rivers, fanned out on our right. To our left, the rising foothills led to wave upon wave of rugged, snowy peaks and ridges, seeming to march endlessly eastward towards Argentina. Periodically, a volcano, lording it over its surroundings, punctuated the jagged mountain chain. Tiny glacial lakes glistened in depressions like emeralds dropped in the snow. At the higher altitudes, proud araucarias or monkey puzzle trees held their prickly heads on long necks high above the snows.

Snatches of my favorite TV weatherman's reports came to mind —

> "In the region of Atacama, sun for breakfast and more for lunch, so don't forget your sunblock."

> "Morning fog will give way to clear skies along the central coast. Get out those picnic baskets."

> "You people in the lakes region will need your umbrellas."

> "In Patagonia, best stay close to the fireplace."

> "Snow flurries in the Antarctic."

> "Easter Islanders can expect partially cloudy skies."

It's no wonder that Chileans refer to their country as the land of *loca geografía*, crazy geography. Where else could you be standing in eighty degree summer heat on a busy city thoroughfare and look up to view glacier topped peaks?

In case we needed reminding that this crazy geography

was in control, one February morning at 3 a.m., we woke to a trembling house. Santiago said, "Did you feel that?"

"Yeah. Another *temblor*," I said. We were used to tremors. This wouldn't last long.

But it grew like a mounting wave. The house rocked as if mounted on a roller coaster. Crashing, rattling sounds came from other rooms. I wondered if I could make it to the dining room to hold up my two china cabinets. But we clutched hands and waited. The swaying grew in intensity, the room tilting and lurching. Finally, we leaped out of bed. I remember saying, "Oh, my God." Earthquakes don't usually frighten me, striking me as fascinating encounters and physical connections with planet Earth. But I'd never experienced anything like this before and I was afraid. We tried the lights. No electricity. I felt my way to the pantry and groped for candles. The movement gradually lessened. The thrusting Nazca Plate and the South American Plate, which meet at Chile's coast, had reached their angle of repose — for now. Our first instinct was to call family, but there was no phone service, water or gas. Batteries were low in the only functioning flashlight. We opened our front door to total darkness and high-pitched ringing of car alarms. Our neighbors across the street appeared in their doorway. Soledad and Andrés from next door came out.

"*Están bien?*" Are you alright?

"Sí." And you? Any damage?"

"We don't know yet."

"That was unbelievable."

Reassuring each other, we returned to our homes. I lit more candles and found batteries for the radio. The news sounded like a series of confused headlines. Tentative. Chaotic.

The neighborhood withstood the quake well. Our house damage was minimum: a broken vase and a glass-framed photo, tumbled CD racks and the television perched precariously at the edge of its stand.

Within a few hours our electricity, gas and water had returned.

SUZANNE ADAM

But, Santiago's sisters and Nico, just blocks away, suffered considerable property damage and continued without the basic services for days.

"Come on over," we said. And they did — for showers, water and use of the refrigerator. Nico and his girlfriend had some Australian friends visiting here, staying in hostels. They arrived with laptops and connected to our Wi-Fi to notify their families that they were well. There was lively conversation of earthquake stories as we gathered around the television to view the scenes of destruction. Though our damage was minimal, for months after the quake I jumped at any loud noise. There's nothing like a good shake-up to impress upon mankind how vulnerable we are in the face of nature.

Chilean Nobel poetess Gabriela Mistral wrote that we live under the cordillera without knowing it, like a crustacean in its shell. She used the word "her" to refer to the Andes Mountains. The Spanish words *cordillera* and *montaña*, are female in gender — so fitting for these multiple breasts of *Pachamama*, Mother Earth, ever present and nurturing — when not teaching us a lesson or two.

The forested Andes of southern Chile, laced with rivers and lakes, fit my original, familiar concept of mountains. But, they are a long day's travel away, and they haven't yet replaced my affections for California's coastal range and the Sierra Nevada. Yet, over the years, the subtle, unique majesty of the stark cordillera viewed from my windows has allowed me to expand my concept of beauty in nature. Continuously, my eyes are drawn to these mountains.

One summer my friend Barbara and a companion came to visit, the first of my American friends to make the long journey. We drove them to the Valle Nevado ski area, the furthest destination on my "beloved road," and though still uneasy with the trip, I wanted to show these sights to my friends. As we ascended to the higher elevations, alpine flowers, fed by melting snow waters, dotted the rocky slopes in pale pink, yellow and lavender hues. The road ended in a wide parking lot, where we gathered up cameras, binoculars and the picnic cooler. In just an hour we'd climbed to over 9,000 feet. We stood in silence, taking in the vastness of the treeless ridges and canyon walls of tilted multi-hued strata. It was dizzying. Condors rode the air currents, seemingly without effort. We could see the white on their upper wings.

A city of now over six million inhabitants was not where I thought I'd settle. I am Aesop's country mouse trapped in the city. Exhaust fumes smother the more delicate scents. The wild grasses where crickets once tuned their fiddles are paved over with cement. The graffiti-covered walls, diminishing open spaces, nerve-jarring car alarms and veils of smog shrouding the cordillera cause me to feel fragile, irritable. I've developed some sharp edges.

Santiago, in its rapid growth and impulse to become a modern city, where the mentality that "bigger is better" reigns and my local supermarket, the Jumbo, has 70 checkout stands, has paid a price. It has lost much of its unique identity, its essence of "Chileness." It could be a city almost anywhere — if it were not for the mountains.

When I was in high school, we took career aptitude tests with questions like: "Would you rather spend your time working with numbers in an office, checking books in a library or hiking in the mountains?" Test results indicated I would make an excellent forest ranger. But I was a late bloomer and couldn't read the signposts.

Perhaps I had to travel the road I did, losing what I had, in order to arrive at the realization that earth, grass, mountain, sky and cloud are my sustenance. Maybe I should have heeded the call of Smokey the Bear. How would I have looked in the brown shorts, khaki blouse and wide hat of a park ranger?

Santiago — the husband — is an urban creature. But, like most Santiago — the city — residents, his childhood roots lay

SUZANNE ADAM

in the campo. His knowledge of birds comes from the summers he spent with his gang of cousins on *Las Brisas*, his mother's farm. Somehow though, he evolved from a slingshot-wielding bird-menace to a savvy, gentle bird-watcher. Everyone we know maintains links with family on farms or in small towns, and weekends and summer days call for a visit. I regret that Santiago's mother's farm is no longer in the family.

This country mouse has had to find ways to come to terms with city existence. I take refuge in my walled garden, poking about, talking to the plants, moving slowly so as not to disturb the doves dining in the grass. The fragrances in my garden, especially after a rain, are precious. I planted many of the flowers whose names I learned as a child — bright marigolds and primroses, delicate azaleas. Early garden experiences help me here when choosing plants and trees at the nursery. I just do an inner switch — similar climates, but opposite hemispheres, opposite seasons. When the azaleas are blooming here, the fragrant wisterias are in flower in the home I left behind.

Central in my stock of city survival strategies have been my walks along city streets, pausing to enjoy the tiny clusters of red fruits on the pepper trees in autumn and the melodic chattering of the wild canaries feeding on seedpods in winter. In spring and summer the flowering trees put on their show: the lilac bursts of the paulonia and the jacaranda, the brash crimson of the ceibo and the soft white catalpa blooms.

Out for a walk one day, I met Marisol. She was selling candy bars at an intersection. Her lithe figure, long dark hair, large eyes and bright smile caught my attention. What was a pretty woman like her doing hawking sweets on a street corner? Her three children romped in the grass in the center strip park. From then on, whenever I walked by, we waved and smiled. Once I stopped to admire her dress. Clearly pleased, she said it was a gift from one of her "*amigas*," as she called the neighborhood señoras who helped her out. Before long, her slim waistline began to swell. "The baby's due in October," she told me. Months later, she was back on the corner, the baby peeking through the folds of a blanket. I soon became one of Marisol's amigas, taking trinkets to the children or sticking a thousand peso bill in my pocket to give her after hearing that she'd been robbed of all her household possessions.

Though Marisol's stories sounded suspiciously melodramatic, maybe because of her warmth and big dark eyes, I believed her. So, too, the one-legged man at the traffic light and the woman with two runny-nosed children outside the supermarket. Other stories I have doubted, having developed inner radar to help me screen out the frauds, though it is not foolproof. Irritated, I shake my head, force a smile and walk by the pleading eyes while guilt tugs at me like an invisible hand.

In the subway station one day, I noticed a large poster that urged: "Smile. It's contagious. We all need love." The next day, while driving, I thought, *it's not easy to smile with my purse wedged between my seat and the car door, stuck in traffic at an intersection where robbers are known to smash rocks though windows to grab unsuspecting ladies' purses.* But I was working on that smile.

One summer afternoon Ann and I explored narrow streets of the old downtown Lastarria neighborhood and lunched at the café where writers hung out. Visiting a thought-provoking photography exhibit, I was moved by the poignancy of the black and white photographs depicting ordinary Chileans involved in their daily activities: a tired waitress standing in a shabby doorway, two men staring blankly at a table filled with empty beer bottles, faces of poverty and hard lives, scenes I seldom witness in our barrio alto bubble.

Only in the city, though, can I thrust a thousand peso bill out the car window in exchange for a plastic bag full of ripe red cherries or plump artichokes. If I need a quick gift or something for the house, I know on which corner I can choose from an assortment of lampshades, deck chairs, sunshades for the car, inflatable toys made in China, musical Santa hats, coat hangers or a rose wrapped in cellophane.

One day, driving along my usual route, I did a double take. Where did that sleek, glass-sided skyscraper come from? It wasn't there the last time I came by. I grieved the loss of the graceful, old, French-style building once standing there before the wrecking ball put an end to its glory. Long gone, too, were the days of our dust-swallowing Fiat. Like so many others, we took advantage of the massive importation of foreign cars.

Apartment towers grow up around us like giant mushrooms, narrowing our view of the mountains. Builders and city planners appear to be blind to the fact that each new tower is another blade whittling away at the slender thread that connects us *Santiaguinos* with this integral piece of our identity. Does ownership of land give unlimited rights to the air and sky above it?

In an increasingly modernized Santiago, a greater variety of options have opened up for me: elongating my muscles at Pilates classes with my Cuban teacher, Alberto; following old Seinfeld episodes on cable TV; cheering on Santiago and my boys in the city's marathon. This is no longer the provincial city that greeted me in 1972.

Yet — how I miss a clear, blue sky overhead and the song of crickets in the night.

Marisol

It is near dark and raining outside, when the doorbell rings. I peek out. A hand waves.

"Hola, Señora Susan. It's me. Marisol." Her daughter, Panchita, is with her.

"What are you doing out in this weather?"

She smiles and tells me she has finished her radiation and chemotherapy treatments.

I compliment her on her spiffy attire: a shiny red raincoat and knee-high beige boots. All donations from her amigas in the neighborhood, she says.

"I'm wearing the sweater you gave me." She pulls up the collar to show me.

"Marisol, how many are living under your roof?"

She names them: five daughters, one granddaughter and one son. Her two older sons are married. She receives a monthly government poverty allotment totaling sixty dollars.

"How can you live on that, Marisol?"

"Well, there's what you and the other señoras give me."

Here's Marisol again, along with Panchita and her toddler Blues. "*Me estoy muriendo*. I'm dying." The latest MRI revealed more cancer. Her face reflects her anguish.

"What are you taking for the pain?" I happen to have some bottles of the medication. "Take some right now." I pass her a spoon. "Have you made arrangements for your children's future?"

"Yes, Blues will go with his father and the older kids with my mother."

They haven't had lunch so I rummage through the pantry and fruit basket.

Today Marisol's stomach is so swollen with tumors, she looks pregnant. There's little flesh on the rest of her. "I'd like to be at home in bed, but we haven't eaten all day." Tears roll down her face.

As if announcing her impending death, she appears dressed in black. Panchita pushes the wheel chair. She asks for herbal tea — all she can get down. I give them some Christmas cookies for the children. She goes into the hospital tomorrow.

This would be the last time I'd see her.

13

No Time to Say Goodbye

Sin decir Adiós

The ring of the telephone ripped into my slumber. I fumbled for the light and glanced at the clock. Two a.m. Probably a prank caller. Or . . . maybe . . . Mother? My hand trembled as I picked up the receiver. It was Chris, Mother's former teaching colleague and our alternate contact person in case of a medical emergency. Dread filled me.

My mother was in the hospital. Pneumonia. I was to call the doctor for more information. They'd contacted Danny in Berkeley and he was on his way to the hospital.

When I got through to the doctor, he explained that pneumonia at her age — two weeks short of her 90th birthday — was tough to beat. Chances were slim that she'd make it through the night. My body shook, but not from cold. We discussed the possibility of fitting her with an oxygen tube, which, if she recovered, she might have to use permanently. I told the doctor that my mother had signed a health directive, indicating she didn't want to have her life prolonged by any mechanical means. Does that include the oxygen tube, I asked? It did. Right at that moment, by telephone, thousands of miles away, I had to make the decision. I asked every question I could think of to help me decide. Finally, I said, no tube.

Danny called around dawn. "Grandma's gone."

Such finality in those two words. I cursed the distance that separated us. I mourned. Why couldn't I have been there with her? To say my good-byes. To hold her hand as she departed this life. Had I ever told her I loved her?

The weeks that followed were a blur: changing plane reservations I'd made to join her for her birthday; Santiago and I scrambling to get the next flight out. I had always known that this moment would come someday and had dreaded it. I'd lived so many years outside the States, how would I know what to do? I no longer knew how things functioned there. I had no American relatives nearby to advise me. Yet, once we arrived, wherever I turned, friends and helpful people appeared. I picked out an outfit for my mother and Santiago accompanied me to the mortuary for a final viewing. I laid my hand on her forehead. It felt so cold.

Nico flew in from Hong Kong where he'd been staying with his girlfriend and her family. Having Santiago and my boys with me eased the burden of sorrow. The members of my mother's church helped me plan the memorial service, which I scheduled for the day of my birthday. Going through a chest of drawers, I found slips of paper with psalms and hymns jotted down. Perhaps she'd left them for me to find, knowing I might need help.

After the service, I slowly and painfully sifted through her possessions, many still packed in boxes from the house move. Santiago kept me company and listened as I talked about the memories contained in yellowed newspaper articles, snapshots, travel brochures, old letters, the familiar sewing basket.

A few days later, I was on my own, Santiago returning to Chile, Nico to Hong Kong, and Danny studying for final exams. One day, going through the cabinet that held my mother's medications, I opened her daily pill dispenser, with the days of the week printed on each lid, one row for a.m. and another for p.m. Panic hit me. She hadn't taken all her medications for two days previous to her death. It was the job of the caregiver to dispense them to her, but the past week there had been yet another change of caregivers. The owner of the agency was supposed to supervise and explain my mother's needs to the new one. Dread, loss and confusion filled me. After thinking it over, I decided to say nothing to the agency owner. What would it accomplish? What had happened? Why hadn't she taken her medication? Had it played a part in her death? I'd never know.

The tasks ahead overwhelmed me. What to do with everything? What should I take to Chile and what should I leave behind forever? The recliner chair would be easy to sell, I thought, putting up signs around the senior residence. I offered my mother's spiffy red walker to 96-year-old Bertha. "Take it for a spin, Bertha," I said. "See how it feels." She loved it. But no takers for the recliner. Even after multiple trips to the Goodwill, I worried what I'd do with my grandmother's desk, my mother's teacup collection, her cherry bedroom set.

The solution came unexpectedly. I suspected Divine Intervention. Danny had just completed his Masters degree and he, Alejandra and the girls were scheduled to move back to Chile, thus also facing a moving dilemma. We were flying back the same day.

He called. "Mom, I heard of this Argentine guy here. He rents containers and makes shipping arrangements. We could send our stuff together."

"You mean ship everything?" I didn't want everything.

"How much?" I knew I'd be paying.

Santiago arranged for Tito, a local Peruvian in the moving business, to pack up the things I'd chosen to keep. For four nights, after work, Tito came round to pack and wrap. He brought his daughter along and I helped with her homework. He even bought my mother's Oldsmobile Cutlass. Things did have a way of working out, though my nights were desolate, sleeping in my mother's bed, surrounded by dark, looming boxes, a carton for a night table. Two days before Christmas, we stuffed the remnants of my parents' lives into a huge orange container already half full with Danny's belongings. We crossed our fingers that we'd see them again someday.

On a rainy afternoon I left Marin County, the most urgent business taken care of. As I drove along the grey, wet freeway, heading to spend Christmas at Danny's student apartment, my mood matched the weather. I was closing a beloved, old book, pulling the curtain across a stage — the stage where our family lived out our lives. I felt cut off from my past. I no longer belonged here.

Three months later the container arrived at the Port of San Antonio aboard the "Clan Legionario." After hours of paper work, we stood on the concrete platform where our container awaited inspection. Trucks and forklifts rumbled past. Agricultural and customs officials hauled out boxes, plastic-wrapped Dora the Explorer bicycles, a Little Tykes kitchen set and the remainders of the two households. The bulky form of the reclining Hulk lurked in the shadows at the back.

"Were the contents fumigated in the States?" one inspector asked.

"Fumigated?" My heart sank. Maybe I could offer him the recliner.

Finally, they signed off and stamped the multiple copies of official papers.

That evening the truck with the container pulled up to our house. In dismay I watched my living and dining rooms fill up with furniture and boxes. I'd need a Houdini to help me through the maze of tape, brown paper and bubble wrap.

I imagined my mother and father laughing and shaking their heads in disbelief at the sight of the towers of boxes and furniture taped in layers of cardboard. I was months unpacking and finding homes for things. I never imagined I would end up here in Chile with so much of the contents of the house on Knoll Road — rubber bands, old coat hangers, carousels filled with slides of past travels.

I'd sell the recliner. I found the perfect spot in the house for some of the pieces of furniture, while others I sold. But the unwanted guest stayed on, waiting, it seemed, for my own decline. When Santiago had surgery, I bought a transformer so he could make use of the chair's reclining features. Then that winter I discovered that the chair, which sat next to a radiator, was the most comfortable one in the house for curling up with a book.

One day I demonstrated the recliner's unique qualities to three-year-old Manuela and Colomba. Their eyes opened wide in fear and mistrust as The Hulk reared up and down like a wooly mammoth. But curiosity won out. I passed them the remote control. That button, I showed them, for *arriba*, the other for *abajo*. Up. Down. Arriba. Abajo.

The girls went for their dolls and blankets and settled into the chair. Hands circling imaginary steering wheels, they drove their great-grandmother's recliner through their make-believe world. "Let's stop at the store," said Manuela. She pressed the button; the motor purred and up and away they went. Then, later, another whirr of the motor and Colomba announced, "Here we are home." I watched them enveloped in that big soft chair and saw my mother sitting there, too.

It was almost as if, unwittingly in small ways, I'd recreated the Adam family home here. Some of the furniture, like the mustard-colored chest with seven drawers, has the scent of our San Anselmo house. Occasionally, I open a drawer and breathe in deeply the fragrance left by the previous contents of the drawers: greeting cards, stationary, pencils, boxes of buttons and spools of thread. My very own time machine.

I knew they were all just *things*, lifeless objects, yet I felt my parents' presence around them. I picked up the small brass watering can and could picture my mother watering her houseplants. I'd wind the old clock every few days, continuing her

SUZANNE ADAM

custom — and my grandmother's, too. In the kitchen, preparing artichokes, I thought: *This is the same knife Mother used.* I was commemorating their lives by placing their things about my home and repeating their rituals.

San Anselmo was not a completely closed chapter. I had to return to take care of legal matters and wanted — needed to go back. But where could I stay? I no longer had a physical place to call *home*, the few friends left in town having no room for me. I sent out feelers. A kind family from my mother's church invited me to stay, saying I'd have a home whenever I wanted to go there. Over the years we would become good friends. What more could I ask for? Right in town, my windows looking out onto a magnificent oak tree, visited by perky grey squirrels. Deer munched on nearby shrubs. At the edge of the garden flowed San Anselmo Creek, where a mallard family swam about.

A therapist once suggested that, in my recurring dreams about houses, a home symbolized the family. In one frequent dream, which began long before my family home was sold, I was deeply distraught seeing strangers living there. In another, the wallpaper in my Chilean home continued to come loose from the wall in big flaps, while I struggled in frustration to stick it back. I also repeatedly dreamt we were back living in our first house here while I wanted to live in the bigger one nearby that we owned (our current home?). I was not sorry to leave that first Santiago house, although we'd lived there twelve years. I tended to remember the difficult times there rather than the good ones. Aside from what my subconscious nocturnal movies might suggest about family relations, I came to realize that I put down my deepest roots in two of the homes in my life: where I spent my childhood and where we live now.

Once the San Anselmo house was sold, the marquis of my dreams was replaced by a sequel of my earlier "Strangers in My House." In "Strangers 2," I was back in Marin on Knoll

Road observing the old family home, though totally changed. I'd creep around on the hill outside, like a peeping Tom, watching some women moving about within. Sometimes I'd sneak inside and wander about without them noticing. How difficult it was for me to let go.

Upon my return to Chile, I felt a strong drive to fix up this house we'd been living in for over twenty-five years. Time for some renovations. Prompted by the acquisitions from California, I threw out the old and shabby and began to make changes, selling our accumulations at garage sales, giving away what wouldn't sell and making trips to the recycling center. Next project: redoing the bathroom. Why so driven at this stage in my life? Maybe it was an inner need to complete the process of making this place home.

At some later point, after those close California ties had been severed, I realized I'd come to terms with the idea of my remains being interred in Chilean soil. With a condition. Like the immigrants buried in Valparaiso's Cementerio de los Disidentes, I want inscribed on my tombstone "Native of California." Yet — I think I'd depart this life in greater peace knowing a portion of the ashes would return north to nourish and mingle with Marin County soil.

April 23, 2010. We were sitting in the bright fall sunlight on the steps of a golf club posing for the family photo — the two families: Senora Olga's and her sister Elena's offspring and spouses, eighty of us. Tiny Señora Olga, dressed in her best blue suit and white blouse with the lace collar, sat in our midst. It was her 100th birthday. Her nineteen great grandchildren squirmed on parents' laps and looked everywhere except at the photographer. Three more great grandchildren were perceptible in the bulges of their mothers' tummies. I looked over the group — my boys, Nico with Andrea, and Danny with Alejandra and their girls, nieces and nephews and, over there, cousin Pablo and his five brothers, filling several rows with their families.

Then I recalled the visceral sensation I felt upon hearing the familiar voices of my father's cousin and his wife, now my closest living relatives in the north, whom I'd called the day before. I knew then that Santiago's family could never replace the family who knew the younger, California me, with whom I shared early memories. But I recognized the deep affection I felt for this large, lively and loving family surrounding me then.

House-sitting

Santiago, a self-declared cat hater, is in an awkward position. For a week we've been in charge of caring for my friend Donna's San Anselmo house, which includes her fluffy, dark-brown cat, Espresso. Thus far, the two are co-habiting with no problems. Santiago is even talking to Espresso, who politely answers. This morning he heard the cat meowing and got up to let him in. Who'd have thought . . .?

One night we hear strange noises at Donna's front door. Santiago opens it to discover big eyes ringed with a black mask staring at us — a hungry raccoon robbing Espresso's food on the porch. I shout at it in Spanish: "*Sale! Sale!*" Oops. English might be more effective. "Shoo! Shoo!" He backs off a bit, but isn't about to give up.

Santiago worries about Espresso who's been sleeping in the garage with the side door open. Raccoons are known to attack cats. He decides to bring the cat and his food inside. Later, the racket continues. The raccoon is now in the garage ripping open a large bag of cat litter. In spite of having no previous raccoon experience, Santiago ousts the marauder from the garage with a broom, securing the door behind him.

This morning, while Santiago is out for a run to Phoenix Lake, I water Donna's garden. It almost feels like I'm living here again as I breathe in the Marin air and the evocative scents, the sun warm on my back.

14

Living Outside the Mountain

Perspectivas

If you are inside a mountain, you cannot see the mountain. This Chinese adage describes the limitations of living solely in one culture. When I read this, it speaks to me. Like the migrating Baird's sandpiper, I live a life of changing perspectives, seldom completely in one place, neither inside nor outside one mountain. Thus, I've often asked myself: are there meaningful reasons for my being here and not there? I can only answer by asking more questions.

Would I ever have stood completely enraptured by the scent of redwoods if I hadn't left? Would I have turned to writing here to explore the shape my life has taken? Was my concept of beauty expanded by the bare Andes visible from my window? Over time, responses have revealed themselves to me. Yet, just when I think I've come to terms, another trip back to my hometown renders the answers fuzzy.

Over the years, on each journey south along the Pan-American Highway, I've absorbed more of this country. During one recent

February excursion, I decided to keep a journal. I wanted to fill in the colors, contours and details of my inner sketch of this landscape.

I was more than ready for my annual nature fix, although a two weeks' sojourn would only satisfy temporarily my hunger for woods and streams.

Santiago and I joined the exodus out of the city. An assortment of vehicles, many of dubious mechanical condition, pushing to the limits the number of passengers for which they were designed — sundry bags, bedding, mattresses, folding chairs and bicycles tied precariously to car roofs, gypsy-fashion — surrounded us on the highway to our destination: the little house at Llifén. This would be our last stay there. The partners in the lakeside venture had subdivided the property. One chose the lot with the house. We selected a lovely piece of land, close to the lake, and talked of building a cabin there someday. But as it was still a thirteen-hour journey, I feared ours was just dream talk.

The day before we left, we'd argued about what stops to make along the way, both of us indecisive, lacking inspiration, wanting the other to decide. Santiago surprised me the next morning, suggesting we take our time, stopping to discover places we'd never seen before — no plan, no reservations, except for our usual stopover at his cousin's cabin on Lake Villarrica.

"Look." I pointed to the bumper of a dilapidated truck: *Solo Dios sabe si vuelvo.* Only God knows if I shall return. "Do you think the driver's fatalism is due to the condition of his truck?"

"Probably."

"I wonder if he noticed the sign back there for Hercules Towing. Sounds as if they could handle any job." I managed to tease a smile onto Santiago's serious face. My chatter was intended to help keep him awake and break up the boredom. I poured coffee from a thermos and offered handfuls of trail mix.

As the melon sun slipped behind the western hills, a road sign ahead read "Constitución 85 kilometers."

"We've never been there," Santiago said, slowing down.

I checked the map. The town was on the coast and not too far. "Fine," I said. Soon it would be dark. Now was a good time to turn off; he was right.

We descended a steep grade overlooking the town's winking yellow lights. At the old Hostería de Constitución we were given the last available room, with lilac walls of textured stucco and a stained, brown carpet. We tried out the two beds. Santiago's came complete with a flea. Flea dispatched, we headed to the hotel's dining room for some local seafood: *ceviche* and sea bass with a shellfish sauce. Then, a familiar voice — Tony Bennett crooning "I Left My Heart in San Francisco." I looked at Santiago and we laughed.

We woke to a bright, sunny day and headed to the dining room for breakfast. The windows looked onto the wide Maule River, dotted with early morning rowers. Our waiter's account of local history reminded me of a conversation I once had with Santiago's mother about her family vacations in Constitución. The climate was good for her mother's health, she said. Her eyes lit up as she described the train trip from Talca and how they'd spend their days: boat rides on the river, horse-drawn buggy rides and walks in the plaza that Santiago and I had wandered through last night. They went there every year until just after her mother died. From a drawer she pulled out a small package of sepia and black and white photos bound with a rubber band, picking out several from her visits to Constitución. One was dated 1924. She was fourteen. Four girls stood at the edge of the foamy surf, dressed in knee-length skirts and long-waisted blouses, each holding a wide-brimmed straw hat. In another, Santiago's mother and her sister were dressed in black. After their mother died, she explained, they wore black for a year, followed by six months of half-mourning in neutral tones of grey and beige. I was grateful to the waiter for allowing me to knit the past to the present.

After a daylight look about, we followed the dirt road south out of town, which skirted the top of ocean cliffs high above beaches of fine black sand. We then turned inland, heading east towards the Andes. Here the dry countryside appeared plain and uninteresting to me. But I wanted to go beyond first impressions and let myself be in that place at that moment to capture its essence — the textures, the scents, the light. What would it be like to live here?

Near the town of Cauquenes, workers in roadside fields were mixing the red soil with water to form bricks and roof tiles. Rows of red tiles, like ones crafted since colonial times by weathered, callused hands, lay in the summer sun to dry, to then be baked in mud ovens like loaves of bread. The old adobe farmhouses and barns that we passed sagged under heavy tile roofs, defying the ravages of weather and earthquakes.

Hours later, the Villarrica volcano was beckoning in the distance. Soon we'd arrive at the lake and Santiago's cousin's cabin. I was fond of the cousins, but wished we could stay at a hotel — nothing fancy — just to have more space, our own bathroom, and to avoid the feeling of freeloading. But I didn't suggest it. Santiago, being more sociable, saw no reason to stay at a hotel when we had an open invitation from relatives.

Ferns and wild fuchsias competed for space along the roadside. In the open green pastures, *bandurrias*, the native ibis, poked their long, curved beaks into the soil in search of insects. Thin wisps of smoke rose from the volcano's snow-flanked fumarole. I practiced pronouncing the names of vacation homes and motels, names borrowed from Mapudungún, the Mapuche language: Tunquelén, Rucantú, Pichimapu, Lelipillán, Huinchatío.

The cousins received us warmly, serving us wine and pisco sours, followed by the traditional barbeque and talk of Chilean poets late into the night. Next day, Santiago and I took off on the last stretch of our journey to our cabin at Lake Ranco.

The road in to the lake from the highway is now paved and lined with impeccably kept dairy farms owned by rich families from the capital. Even the cows looked clean, their black and white attire sharply contrasting with the deep green of the fields. Past the town of Llifén, we entered the wooden gate that enclosed the cabin and its grounds. The caretaker, Daniel, his wife, Cristina, their children and their dogs came out to greet us. The dogs were a touchy issue between us and Daniel and Cristina, the scraggly canine greeting committee of mixed heritage growing yearly. We, the owners, but strangers to the dogs, expected wagging tails upon arrival; instead, we encountered suspicious snarls. We asked that they tie up the least friendly dog but he was an escape artist, finding no better place to nap than the mat at our front door.

I spent the first day stretched out on the warm, smooth rock formation at the end of the beach, listening to the water's lapping, and watching a blue, white and russet kingfisher slicing into the water after its prey. Memories of past family vacations came back to me. Perhaps the summer days spent here influenced my boys' decisions to pursue work in environmental fields. Now, I've released them into the world where I hope their own perspectives, built on a bi-national upbringing, travels and studies abroad, allow them to cross cultural and linguistic borders with understanding.

The next afternoon, friends arrived. At dusk we took our glasses of wine to the deck to watch the liquid sun slip below the western rim of the lake. I warned them, "Tonight in bed you'll hear shuffling, squeaking noises overhead. They're just the resident bats." Soon, shadowy shapes began darting from under the eaves of the roof. I counted and, after several minutes, announced, "Seventy-three. More or less."

"And we sleep under the same roof?" my amiga Gena asked.

"Don't worry. They've never gotten into the house."

We entertained ourselves talking, laughing, eating, and sleeping, followed by more talking and laughing and eating. I almost felt like one of them. I understood the jokes and plays on words, even making a few myself, and was prepared when one of my mispronunciations produced howls of laughter.

Someone said, "You have an excellent vocabulary. It's the

pronunciation that frustrates you." Yes, that accent is my life-term ball and chain.

As our friends prepared to leave, Gena commented, "You're the best-adapted foreigner I've ever known."

"Do you know any others?" I asked.

She laughed. "Well — no."

"*No importa*," I said. "No matter. *Gracias*." Her observation surprised and pleased me.

The next morning, I walked towards the Calcurrupe River as I had so many times over the years, greeting the wild alstroemeria on the hillsides, scanning the blackberry bushes for ripe fruit, watching for an elusive *chucao* bird who laughed at me from the underbrush — all that I'd hungered for in the long months of city life.

The scene at the river's edge was no longer as I remembered. The *balsa*, or ferry, was gone. Ferry was really too grand a name; raft was more like it. It held two or three cars or a large lumber truck, plus assorted bicycles, pedestrians and animals. Two men, wearing heavy gloves, used poles to push away from shore, and then pulled on a thick, grinding cable attached to an overhead line to make the five-minute crossing. From the riverbank, I watched campesinos on the opposite shore lining up large milk containers, loading them onto the balsa to deliver them to the waiting truck. Sometimes I hopped on, just for the ride.

But progress had reached isolated Llifén. The road was now paved to the river and, instead of the balsa, a steel and concrete bridge had been erected. Yet, the water still flowed an almost transparent green, and I felt its breezes brushing my face. The words to an old Girl Scout song came to mind: *Peace I ask of thee, Oh River, peace, peace, peace.*

Returning to the big city, I had little time to grieve the tranquil, lush landscape we'd left behind. The threat of the construction of a mall just blocks from our house catapulted me into a whirl of activity. A large chain of department stores and supermarkets had purchased a tract of land, previously destined for educational use. The company planned to request a change of the zoning regulations. The mayor declared he would let a plebiscite among the residents decide the matter. I joined members of our neighborhood association, walking door to door with leaflets, marching with placards, blowing whistles and shouting through a bullhorn, "*No al mall! No al mall!*" We made use of Internet. At first, the press paid us little attention. OK, we said, let's stop traffic. The green vans of the *carabineros* appeared, and fast upon their heels, the press and television cameras. The company launched its own all-out campaign.

One evening, in an out-of-body moment, I watched myself sitting with three women in my neighbor's kitchen, planning our next move, but with each glass of wine, the conversation strayed to more entertaining topics. I looked around me and thought, *maybe* I've finally arrived.

It was David against Goliath, but grass roots democracy won out against big money. Our neighborhood established a precedent for the right of ordinary citizens to be heard in decisions regarding the destiny of their environs. And I was rediscovering a latent interest for civic concerns and an outlet for my environmental passions. I felt a growing urgency to contribute to making this a greener, more humane city.

My graceful redwood, visible outside my window, comforts me. It is my companion in this life-shaping journey. Though we will always be "introduced species," year after year, our roots push deeper into Chilean soil.

SUZANNE ADAM

The Visit

One hundred-and-three years-old, Señora Olga chose the early hours of Christmas Eve to die. Had she timed it to bring all three generations of cousins, nieces, nephews, aunts and uncles together at Christmas?

Nervousness rippled through the crowd gathered outside Santa Elena Church. The doors were padlocked closed and no sign of the priest. More people arrived, milling about on the sidewalk. We checked our watches and asked:

"What happened to the priest or his attendant?"

"Go around the side and ring the doorbell."

"Did you find the priest?"

"He must be asleep."

Finally, the lights went on inside and the doors opened. The priest and the keys had been found.

Sorrow of loss, tears and laughter marked the delayed funeral service. Although she'd left the world of the living, Señora Olga remained with us in her legacy of twenty-two great-grandchildren, several of whom were curious about the long wooden box where "Ita" lay. They'd venture up to peer at the coffin, and then run back to mommy, first one, and then another. Little Agustina, the most persistent, was intrigued by a white tassel of silk that protruded from the casket, tugging at it in spite of her mother's admonishments.

This morning a turtle dove wandered through our open kitchen door. When I entered, the dove flew up, startled, and flapped wildly against the window. I moved slowly towards it, cupped it in my hands and released it into the backyard.

I said to Santiago, "Maybe that was a visit from your mother."

He smiled. "She always liked to wander about our garden."

Epilogue

It was a holiday, Columbus Day, *Día de la Raza*, in Chile — a fitting date for my excursion. The day shone bright and clear, and the cordillera called to me. My hands gripped the steering wheel. It was my first time driving this zigzag road on my own. The yellow sign on the switchback ahead read number 14. Thank God, only one more to go. Rounding the bend, I glanced at the steep drop plunging to the canyon far below. At curve 15, I turned in at the wooden gate of the Yerba Loca Nature Sanctuary and headed to a small parking area.

Just as climbing Marin County's Mt. Tamalpais bonded me closely to that landscape of rocky trails, scrubby manzanita and redwood groves, I now hoped to create a greater intimacy with this mountainous terrain.

A trail sloped gently through the narrow valley, never far from a rushing river, pregnant with melting snow. On a hillside ahead, gnarled fruit trees and crumbling stone walls were the only signs of previous human habitation. Someone had named this place Villa Paulina. Maybe a house stood here at one time, these low winding stones remnants of corrals. Bright white blossoms on fruit trees contrasted sharply with the azure sky. I'd read that the trees were planted by the previous owners of the land, a German family.

The distant peak of *La Paloma*, The Dove, beckoned me, promising ancient glaciers and hidden secrets. A covey of quail scattered into the underbrush at my approach, twittering in alarm. Bare stone valley walls, etched with cracks and crevices, resembled the browned, weathered faces of old mountain men, a jutting chin here, a brow there, still and solemn in silent wisdom.

I was in no hurry. The being here was all.

I settled on a rock by a rivulet making its way down the mountainside, and inhaled the clean mountain air, scented with the breath of shrubs and water on rocks. Birds alighted on soggy patches of new, green grass, springtime oases in the rocky terrain. The valley and its enormous silence enveloped me. Only the trickling of water and the call of a bird punctuated the stillness.

Some days later, I encountered my German friend Fanny and told her about my excursion to Yerba Loca. Her house sat on a mountaintop rising from the start of the winding road. Her faded blue eyes lit up.

"The valley belonged to my father-in-law," she said. "The stone walls are the remains of the house where I spent my summers, years ago. But we had to leave."

I pictured her children wandering freely in that wild expanse.

"What happened?" I asked.

"The government expropriated the land."

"The fruit trees were in bloom," I told her.

She smiled. "Ah, yes, the almond trees." After a pause, she added, "I haven't been back in many years."

"Don't you miss the place?"

"My dear, I am not attached to anything anymore. I'm happy

to have spent that time there and to have those memories, but I'm pleased that other people can enjoy it now."

Fanny's wise words were still fresh in my mind during my next trip to California. "I want to go by the house," I said to Santiago.

"What for? That's in the past now."

I knew he also loved the house, yet his words sounded harsh and unfeeling. The old neighbourhood was as familiar as a childhood friend. I walked slowly towards the house and contemplated its façade, its garden and the trees I once climbed. I hoped the new owners wouldn't object to a woman standing on the road outside. On the deck above, a blonde woman was sweeping. A man joined her.

The pair of cycling pants hung out to dry on a rack in front of the house decided me. If there was a cyclist in the family, they'd be friendly and receptive. I rang the doorbell. A handsome man, grimy in gardening clothes, answered the door. I explained who I was and told him the cycling pants were my goad. He was the cyclist, he said. Two excited dachshunds jumped at me. The blonde woman came to the top of the stairs and invited us in. She was interested in knowing about the house and knew the original owners had been named Adam. We climbed the steps in the back garden and I pointed to the cobblestone wall. "My father built that." She showed me where they were planning to put in a hot tub. I offered to make copies of photos of the original lot and the house under construction to bring to her next time. I wanted an excuse to come back and for them to know the history of the house, so that the memory of our family might endure, our spirits welcome there.

In Chile, memories of redwoods, the strident squawks of blue jays, the fragrance of the tarweed continue to tug at me, and I know I'll return whenever the possibility presents itself, but I continuously remind myself to live in the here and the now.

One morning, the year's first snowfall having occurred during the night, I looked out my window at the glorious Andes cloaked in bridal white.

I called to Santiago. "Come see the mountains!"

Acknowledgments

This memoir was a long time in the making, a journey within a journey, and, thus my gratitude extends to the many travelers who accompanied me along the way. My muses throughout have been the natural worlds of California and Chile and their people.

I am indebted to my colleagues of the Santiago Writers for their endless patience, encouragement and gentle critiquing. I am especially grateful to Sue Siddley for organizing her workshops at Los Parronales farm every summer.

Mil gracias to my son, Nicolás, for his whimsical illustrations and to Juan Pablo Calabi for the resplendent cover photo.

Many thanks to Peace Corps Writers and, especially to Marian Haley Beil, who made it possible for this book to see the light of day.

I also wish to thank Canadian editor and writing instructor, Allyson Latta for her invaluable input and California-based writer/writing instructor Laura Deutsch.

Loving thanks to my husband, Santiago, without whom this would have been a different story.

Made in the USA
Middletown, DE
18 August 2018